twinkle's town & country knits

30 designs for sumptuous living

WENLAN CHIA

POTTER CRAFT

NEW YORK

Dedication

This book is dedicated to my parents, Hungyeh Chia and Chuyin Chia, and my husband, Bernard Lin. You inspire me daily to nurture a life of creativity.

Published in the United States by Potter Craft, an imprint of the Crown Publishing Group, a division of Random House, Inc., New York.
www.crownpublishing.com
www.pottercraft.com

POTTER CRAFT and CLARKSON N. POTTER are trademarks, and POTTER and colophon are registered trademarks of Random House, Inc.

Library of Congress Cataloging-in-Publication Data is available

ISBN 978-0-307-34612-4

Printed in China

Design by Lauren Monchik
Photography by Michael Crouser

Thanks to the Craft Yarn Council of America (www.yarnstandards.com) for their Standard Yarn Weight System Chart, which appears on page 153.

10   9   8   7   6   5   4   3   2   1

First Edition

CREDITS

STYLIST Sharon Anderson

PHOTOGRAPHER Michael Crouser

WRITER AND EDITORIAL CONSULTANT John Haffner Layden

INSTRUCTION WRITER Edie Eckman

TECHNICAL EDITOR Charlotte Quiggle

MAKEUP ARTIST Sara Gelman for NARS

HAIR STYLIST David Cruz for REDKEN

MODELS Martina Correa, Ciara Nugent, and Hanne Gaby Odiele

CASTING MAO PR

SPECIAL CAMEO Milan

twinkle's town & country knits

30 designs for sumptuous living

WENLAN CHIA

NEW YORK

highlander's stole

This lavish basketweave stole balances the riot of color and pattern in Ciara's ensemble and embellishes it with a touch of classic luxury. For more casual affairs, rock this wrap with a sparkly pin and wear it over a lightweight vintage-style floral print dress along with a pair of D'Orsay snakeskin pumps.

page 50

greetings

FROM GLAMOURTOWN

The house of fashion, we all know, is built on fantasy. It would be a mistake, though, to underestimate this foundation. A potent alloy of imagination, aspiration, and identification, fantasy has bolstered revolutionary movements and fueled epic creations. Its power and value are profound. A daily dose of fantasy injects a much-needed measure of excitement and joy into our routines. So why do some dismiss it as an extravagance of daydreamers and romantics? Perhaps they've mistaken pleasure for profligacy or just forgotten that compromises can be struck. In the right degree, fantasy can inspire us to live more richly than we ordinarily might. As with most things in life (including fashion), it's a matter of proportion and balance. But as you thumb through this chapter, take my advice and tip the scale to the side of romance, fun, and glamour.

The patterns in this chapter herald the appeal of town holidays. On an urban vacation, take a leisurely pace through your day to slow the city's hectic tempo. There's time to study the soaring steeples above your head or survey the local gallery scene. Twinkle gals sport versatile knits attuned to a city setting, whether they're dressing up for a film premiere, stopping by a social gathering in an historic home, or dropping in on friends at cocktail hour. The breathtaking Belle du Jour Tunic (page 14), which features sexy openwork formed by rows of dropped-stitch ladders—a Twinkle trademark—is a complete look all by itself. Accessories such as the Vauxhall Poet's Scarf (page 17) or the Highlander's Stole (page 10), in contrast, complement outfits built on other garments. You'll also learn to work "Criss-Cross Cables" and two wavy stripe stitch patterns.

on page 148. Look for knitting tips, called "Twinkle Knit Bits," scattered among the patterns. Don't forget, too, that knitting with friends is another great way to share tips, try out new patterns, explore color palettes, and check the fit of garments in progress.

Speaking of fit, you've probably noticed that many of my patterns take a playful approach to shape and scale. Rather than focus on complex stitches, I highlight fit and silhouette in Twinkle by Wenlan designs. Many feature a flattering, form-hugging shape that looks modern and sexy, especially in bulky yarns. (Know, too, that my yarns are soft enough to wear against your skin or over tissue-thin layers—they're not the scratchy wools of long ago.) Rest assured that a lot of care has gone into calculating proper fit. Use your bust measurement as a general guide to selecting the right size to make, but remember that every body is different. Check your hip and waist measurements against the schematics and pattern headnotes, where I often offer how-to notes for choosing the correct size for the best fit. If you see measurements on a schematic that are smaller than those of your body, trust that I've adjusted the pattern for ease with the yarns and stitches in mind.

Throughout this book, use the following guide to correlate your bust measurement to size:
XS = 31"-33" (78.5cm-84cm);
S = 34"-36" (86cm-91.4cm);
M = 37"-39" (94cm-99cm);
L = 40"-42" (101.6cm-106.7cm).
When calculating finished garment dimensions from gauge measurements, we rounded up or down as needed to make the range between sizes uniform. It isn't a problem if your finished measurement is off by a half-inch; the pattern and yarns are forgiving.

Extra thought was given to pattern construction to ensure that pieces can be seamed cleanly for trim, sleek silhouettes. Likewise, chunky knit designs sometimes demand special techniques such as asymmetrical bind-offs on sleeves or decreases on both the front and back of garments for tailored shaping. Anticipate these particular steps, and familiarize yourself with a piece's construction by studying the pattern carefully before beginning the project. Responses from my savvy test knitters suggest that some of the instructions you'll read may include steps you're not used to seeing in pattern books. I'd like to think that what sets Twinkle by Wenlan patterns apart is the experimentation put into designing solutions that yield the most flattering, bespoke results.

The patterns in *Twinkle's Town & Country Knits* offer some sublime fashions to enliven your wardrobe with luxurious "town and country" looks that become wholly your own. Cardigans that at first seem classic and familiar reveal unexpected, romantic twists to make you stand out from the crowd. Scarves with uncommon proportions and details will delight. Ribbed waists and necklines complement every body. That's the secret of Twinkle sumptuous living: eye-catching, wearable clothes possessing a signature whimsical charm and wit. It may be a signature of the Twinkle life, but it's a life that awaits you, too!

introduction

People often ask me about presenting the seasonal collections of Twinkle by Wenlan, my fashion company, during Fashion Week in New York City. When they do, I sometimes deliver an amusing story of a behind-the-scenes crisis or report a celebrity sighting. Fashion Week certainly offers an ideal backdrop for some serious drama: juggling eleventh-hour changes to the model bookings, handling last-minute alterations, and coping with the logistical hurdles of creating a total look for the show, to name a few. Listeners are usually surprised to learn, though, that the really exciting drama, for me, has to do with the exuberance and cheery, youthful smiles of the models backstage who slip into my knitwear and are delighted to find how comfy and fun it is to wear. Cozied up in a cardigan or pullover, awaiting their turn on the runway, they look as if they're on their way to some romantic, glamorous, fabulous event that you and I would enjoy, too. Those moments capture the spirit of sumptuous living that I imagine when I think of the Twinkle gal and her world.

Knits figure perfectly into the luxurious lifestyle of the fabled Twinkle gal partly because knitwear suits the point of view and pursuits of the modern woman who not only enjoys life but takes pleasure in our shared craft as well. Like you and me, this imaginary Twinkle muse needs clothes that keep pace with contemporary life—with its parties, outings, casual get-togethers, and dressy events. Her fashion philosophy isn't one that promotes a studied, overwrought look; rather, it's eclectic in style, inspired by art and nature, and improvised instead of inflexible. Tossing together the vintage with the new, the precious with the everyday, and the romantic with the edgy, she ends up with the whimsical, romantic style for which my collections are known. But she also needs hip patterns to knit! The designs in this knitwear book and my previous ones, taken from Twinkle by Wenlan collections, offer charming, luxurious contributions to that style and unique opportunities to expand a knitter's skills. (Many of the patterns call for super-chunky yarns, so they knit up in a flash for wearing or gift-giving, too.)

So, isn't it about time you absorbed a little of the Twinkle charm by paging through *Twinkle's Town & Country Knits*? When choosing patterns for this collection, "town and country" became the touchstone phrase I returned to again and again. Something about the richness—and perhaps the elusive mystery—of the aristocratic, romantic, and sophisticated life those words evoked seemed to agree with the Twinkle definition of sumptuous living. To me, "town and country" suggests a lifestyle in which each part—the urban and the pastoral—complements the other in a harmonious whole. I think that for most of us, having a little of each kind of energy results in a soothing balance. And to enjoy a place in both landscapes—isn't that the ultimate in sumptuous living? In a way, the Twinkle way of dressing evolves from a similar kind of balance of elements, modernizing the casually assembled, offhand chic of women who embodied the "town and country" look of years past.

Follow the migrations of the fabulously photographed Twinkle gals, chapter by chapter: The scene changes but not the mood—fun and adventure prevail as they vacation in town, holiday in the countryside, or shuttle 'round a resort. Captured in the midst of some glamorous goings-on, these girls are practiced in the art of living. In fact, they are the living definition of Twinkle sumptuous living. The pleasures of travel, one of life's great luxuries and a touchstone of this book, inspired these pictures. To celebrate travel, tips I've collected are sprinkled throughout the book. Note, too, that the photo captions offer styling suggestions based on the Twinkle look to help you assemble outfits for any occasion and choose a first pattern to work.

Twinkle's Town & Country Knits offers knitters of all skill levels projects to enjoy and incorporate into their wardrobes. Along the way, you'll learn some new ways to shape knit garments and work large-scale stitches into tailored looks. Soon, you'll be borrowing my techniques to create your own patterns, carrying knitwear design into fresh territory. For help mastering stitches and techniques, newer knitters can refer to the Tips and Techniques section

table of contents

gitane tunic dress

The scooped neck and sensual waves of color that undulate around the hem and sleeves of the Gitane Tunic Dress evoke a 1960s peasant dress from the Mediterranean. Here, a vintage metal belt adds shimmer and defines the nipped waist formed by snug ribbing. Make this dress street-worthy by wearing it over a turtleneck with jeans and stylized engineer boots.

page 52

belle du jour tunic

This sexy mohair shift showcases both your knitting technique and your figure. Vertical cables run the length of this princess-line tunic and become shoulder straps, bordering the lacy dropped-stitch ladders. The openwork allows the garment worn beneath to show through. So you can wear it over a nude-colored slip for a daring "barely there" look or choose a color or pattern that contrasts with the dark knit. Almost an accessory, this knit can glam up a dress, or be a weekend look: Slip it over skinny black jeans and a black tank and wear with flats or flat knee-high boots.

page 54

metropolitan diary skirt

Hanne illustrates Twinkle style in her collage of tailored wovens over a softly colored romantic knit. The boldly scaled fluted hem lends movement, and decreases on the front form an elegant tapering detail. Accented by modern charms dangling from chains, this look recalls the chic "town and country" set of generations past but in a fresh, new way. It's perfect for cocktails and gallery openings. If your idea of sumptuous living is more T-Rex than tea dance, contrast this flirty skirt with a vintage rock T-shirt and ballet flats or knee-high, lace-up moccasins.

page 57

vauxhall poet's scarf

A special stitch pattern gives this stylish muffler a regular pattern of subtle vertical stripes that bracket twists of yarn and eyelets. This lighter, more feminine, version of a schoolboy scarf elongates the silhouette of the floor-length dress Ciara wears and introduces a burst of color. The scarf's perforations smartly echo the eyelet fabric of the dress. On a brisk fall day, wear it to a café over a camel or navy peacoat along with dressy cords and platform sandals with textured socks.

page 59

urban legend skirt

A luxurious, glamorously long skirt makes an indelible impression as Hanne relaxes before the evening's party. The Urban Legend falls in elegant waves of harmonious tones that mirror the delicately shaped neckline of her tiered silk blouse. Where the waves rise in the Feather and Fan Stripes pattern, playful openings hint at what's concealed below. Cool colors in coordinating hues also would work well for the flared skirt's swaying bands. For a trip into town, pull on some well-worn Frye boots and top the skirt with a simple white T-shirt and a favorite denim jacket.

page 60

weaver's cardigan

As pretty as it is practical, this cardi is snug and charming with its raised princess line flanked by bobbles and buttons marching down the front. Worked mainly in purl, matching dashes edge the wide stripes to enliven the pattern. The casual stand-up collar suggests sportswear. Here, Twinkle's print-on-pattern styling philosophy has Hanne in a chunky knit layered over a festive, flowing dress for a look that's feminine but not precious. When the occasion calls for pants, try dark, over-dyed jeans and ankle boots. In cooler climes? Tuck jeans into knee-high boots, and button the Weaver's

matinee coat

A ruffle attached to the buttonhole edge shimmies down the front of this extravagant knit, swaying in time to Hanne's playful flamenco solo. The cool hues and fluid movement of her voluminous silk skirt keep tempo with the Matinee Coat's dramatic detailing. A bold profile emerges from the asymmetrical double-breasted front opening, exaggerated pouch pockets, and full, short, dropped sleeves drawn in at the cuff. A subdued, classic palette makes this knit ideal for urban outings, while its purl construction gives it a handcrafted, relaxed feel. So don't be afraid to dress it down by playing off the slouchy, chic silhouette with charcoal velvet straight-leg trousers and bright satin pumps.

page 66

a country

ESTATE OF MIND

If city life is made up of verticals—cloud-cloaked skyscrapers, express elevators, and ramped-up energy levels—then country life is all about the horizontals—expanses of glittering lakes, drawn-out dinners on the veranda, and unfurling horizons. Your sense of space and freedom grows as you leave the highways to meander down lanes flanked by fields and forests. Nature makes its presence known with seasons that set the pace of country living. A country retreat offers a chance to surrender to those rhythms and the peace and quiet they afford. It also presents opportunities for pleasures you can't easily indulge in the city, like spending the day cooking foods fresh from the farm stand for a laid-back dinner party, taking some riding lessons, or finally polishing off that novella.

In Chapter 2, the Twinkle gals play host to visitors at the country manor. Their wardrobe: Comfy accessories for *plein-air* jaunts to markets, and sweater dresses, pullovers, and a knee-skimming cardi for outdoor pursuits. With the Middlebury Scarf (page 24), you'll have the perfect opportunity to practice short rows; the Bennington Jumper Dress (page 30) invites you to try your hand at intarsia.

new haven hat and middlebury scarf

In this comfy cap made from soft, supple Twinkle wool, Martina looks as fresh as the produce surrounding her. Bold cables cage the crown of the New Haven hat, whose cheery color alone could keep her warm. Below it, pleats of featherweight yellow mohair ripple on the Middlebury Scarf, a study in short-row shaping with a delicate, crocheted edge. Embodying the unstudied, casual Twinkle mode of dressing, the scarf is worn with a fitted intarsia knit under a belted, short-sleeved print dress. Complete the look with tights and platform Mary Janes and top it off with a camel A-line coat.

new haven hat page 72;
middlebury scarf page 74

bar harbor hoodie vest

The sinuous, sensuous lines of this knit are created by the subtle roll of the collar as it lengthens into a hood, the outsized pockets, and decreases at the waist and ribbing at the hem to narrow the fit. The dropped-armhole cap sleeves, cuffed and buttoned, are a refined detail. Here, Martina tops a richly colored, geometric print silk blouse, a pair of earth-toned, flared shorts, and faintly striped tights with the hoodie, buttoning it only at the top to create a vibrant combination of lines, textures, and colors. Perfect for layering over faded jeans and a thermal underwear shirt for weekend fun, it boasts a curvy shape that complements graceful, flowing dresses for dressier affairs as well.

page 76

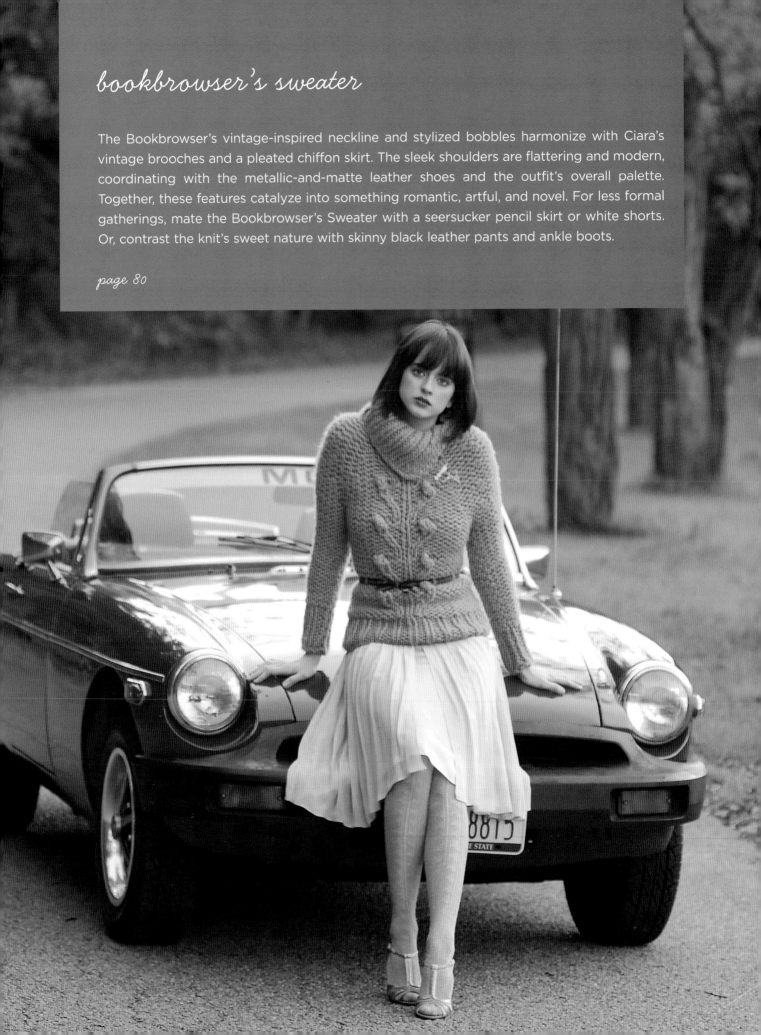

bookbrowser's sweater

The Bookbrowser's vintage-inspired neckline and stylized bobbles harmonize with Ciara's vintage brooches and a pleated chiffon skirt. The sleek shoulders are flattering and modern, coordinating with the metallic-and-matte leather shoes and the outfit's overall palette. Together, these features catalyze into something romantic, artful, and novel. For less formal gatherings, mate the Bookbrowser's Sweater with a seersucker pencil skirt or white shorts. Or, contrast the knit's sweet nature with skinny black leather pants and ankle boots.

page 80

millbrook sweater dress and vineyard potter's cardigan

This multipurpose pair of chunky knits ushers you down country lanes or into chic upstate restaurants. Meandering cables with bobbles and contrasting stitches on the Millbrook Sweater Dress accentuate the figure. The Vineyard Potter's Cardigan is at once traditional and modern. Ribs at the hem wander out of alignment to become the pretty latticework of the cardi's front section.

STOLE

Using cable cast-on method, cast on 30 stitches. Work even in Criss-Cross Cables Pattern until the piece measures approximately 50" (127cm) from the beginning, ending with Row 4 of the pattern.

Bind off loosely. Weave in ends.

CRISS-CROSS CABLES STITCH CHART

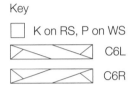

Key

☐ K on RS, P on WS

⬛ C6L

⬛ C6R

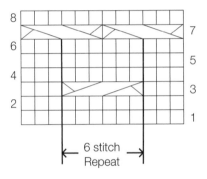

← 6 stitch Repeat →

Repeat shifts 3 sts on Row

gitane tunic dress

page 12

The springy silk-and-cotton Cruise yarn makes an elastic fabric, especially when knitted with four strands held together. This is ideal for a pattern such as this one, which requires a snug section that holds the garment firmly to the body in order to accommodate other elements that have movement and fullness. The Wavy Stripes Pattern—a combination of pairs of stitches knitted together and yarn overs—draws together stitches and creates openness between others, coaxing the hemline and stripes into charming undulations. The raglan shoulder shaping and stretchy knit give this dress a comfortable fit.

SIZES

XS (S, M, L)

Remember to use this guide to find your size based on your bust measurement: XS = 31"–33" (79cm–84cm); S = 34"–36" (86cm–91cm); M = 37"–39" (94cm–99cm); L = 40"–42" (102cm–107cm).

KNITTED MEASUREMENTS

Bust: 30$\frac{1}{2}$ (32, 33$\frac{1}{2}$, 35$\frac{1}{4}$)" (77.5 [81, 85, 89.5]cm)

Back length (to neck): 24 (24$\frac{3}{4}$, 25$\frac{1}{4}$, 26)" (61 [63, 64, 66]cm)

MATERIALS

10 (11, 12, 13) balls Twinkle Handknits Cruise, 70% silk/30% cotton, 1$\frac{3}{4}$ oz/50g, 120 yds/109m, #09 Black (A) and 4 (5, 5, 6) balls, #45 River (B) 2

US size 15 (10mm) 24" (60cm) circular needle or size needed to obtain gauge

Stitch holders

Stitch markers

Tapestry needle

GAUGE

12 stitches and 17 rows = 5$\frac{1}{2}$" (14cm) in Wavy Stripes Pattern with four strands held together on size 15 (10mm) needle.

Take the time to check your gauge.

ABBREVIATION

Dec 1 (decrease 1): K2tog or p2tog as necessary to maintain rib pattern.

Wavy Stripes Pattern (multiple of 12)

ROWS 1 AND 3 (WS): With A, purl.
ROW 2: With A, *(k2tog) 4 times, (yo, k1) 4 times; repeat from * across.
ROW 4: With A, knit.
ROWS 5–8: With B, repeat Rows 1–4.
Repeat rows 1–8 for pattern.

The entire piece is worked with four strands of yarn held together. Work flat pieces back and forth on circular needle, carrying unused color loosely along the side edge. First, the sleeves are knit flat. The body is knit flat to the beginning of the ribbing, then joined and worked in the round to the underarms. The sleeves are joined to the body at the underarm, and the sweater is knit in one piece in the round from that point. Mark the beginning of the round with a stitch marker in a different color from the others.

SLEEVES (MAKE 2)

With 4 strands of A held together, and using long-tail cast-on method, cast on 48 (48, 60, 60) stitches.

Begin Wavy Stripes Pattern and work 16 rows even, ending with Row 8 of the pattern.

NEXT ROW (WS): Decrease as follows:
SIZES XS AND S ONLY: ★P2tog, p4 (6); repeat from ★ across.
SIZE M ONLY: ★(P2tog, p2) 3 times, p2tog, p1; repeat from ★ 3 times.
SIZE L ONLY: ★(P2tog, p2) 5 times, (p2tog, p3) 2 times; repeat from ★ once more.
ALL SIZES: Bind off 2 stitches at the beginning of the next 2 rows—36 (38, 40, 42) stitches remain. Place these stitches on a holder.

BODY

With 4 strands of A held together, and using long-tail cast-on method, cast on 120 (120, 132, 132) stitches.

Begin Wavy Stripes Pattern and work 24 rows.

Repeat Rows 1–4 only of Wavy Stripes Pattern for 24 more rows. Do not turn at the end of the last row;

place marker to indicate beginning of round.

Continuing in the round with right side facing, decrease as follows:

SIZE XS ONLY: ★(K2tog, k1) 3 times, k2tog; repeat from ★ 9 times, end (k2tog, k1) 2 times, (k2tog) 2 times.
SIZE M ONLY: ★(K2tog, k1) 3 times, k2tog; repeat from ★ 11 times.
SIZES S AND L ONLY: ★K1, k2tog; repeat from ★ around.
ALL SIZES: 76 (80, 84, 88) stitches remain.

Change to k1, p1 rib (see page 00) and work 6 rounds even.

NEXT RND: Dec 1, work 34 (36, 38, 40) stitches in k1, p1 rib as established, dec 1, place marker to indicate right underarm, dec 1, work in rib as set to last 2 stitches, dec 1—72 (76, 80, 84) stitches.

Work 8 rounds even; end last round 2 stitches before end of round.

NEXT RND: Removing markers, bind off 4 stitches, work to 2 stitches before next marker, bind off 4 stitches, work to end—32 (34, 36, 38) stitches on each of Front and Back.

JOIN SLEEVES AND BODY

NEXT RND: Continuing in rib as established, work across 36 (38, 40, 42) Left Sleeve stitches, place marker for left front raglan shaping, work across 32 (34, 36, 38) Front stitches, place marker for right front raglan shaping, work across 36 (38, 40, 42) Right Sleeve stitches, place marker for right back raglan shaping, work across 32 (34, 36, 38) Back stitches, place marker for left back raglan shaping and end of round—136 (144, 152, 160) stitches.

Work 1 round even.

RAGLAN SHAPING

NEXT RND (DEC RND): ★K1, ssk, work to 2 stitches before marker, k2tog; repeat from ★ around—128 (136, 144, 152) stitches.

Repeat Dec Rnd on every other round 3 (4, 2, 3) times more, then every 3rd round 1 (1, 3, 3) time(s) more —96 (96, 104, 104) stitches remain.

Bind off in pattern.

FINISHING

Sew sleeve, side, and underarm seams. Weave in ends.

GITANE TUNIC DRESS SCHEMATIC

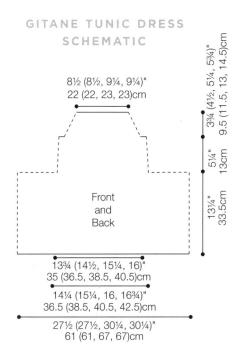

8½ (8½, 9¼, 9¼)"
22 (22, 23, 23)cm

3¾ (4½, 5¼, 5¾)"
9.5 (11.5, 13, 14.5)cm

5¼"
13cm

Front and Back

13¼"
33.5cm

13¾ (14½, 15¼, 16)"
35 (36.5, 38.5, 40.5)cm

14¼ (15¼, 16, 16¾)"
36.5 (38.5, 40.5, 42.5)cm

27½ (27½, 30¼, 30¼)"
61 (61, 67, 67)cm

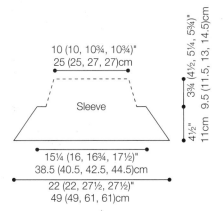

10 (10, 10¾, 10¾)"
25 (25, 27, 27)cm

3¾ (4½, 5¼, 5¾)"
9.5 (11.5, 13, 14.5)cm

Sleeve

4½"
11cm

15¼ (16, 16¾, 17½)"
38.5 (40.5, 42.5, 44.5)cm

22 (22, 27½, 27½)"
49 (49, 61, 61)cm

belle du jour tunic

page 14

This arresting tunic is worked with two strands of mohair held together. Owing to the yarn's dark color and texture, as well as the great number of cast-on stitches, you may want to work with a light-colored cloth spread on your lap to make the stitches more visible—especially when it's time to join the cast-on stitches into a round. The pattern relies on a Cable 8 Left sequence to produce the twined "ropes" that stabilize the edges of the dropped-stitch ladders and become the shoulder straps. Your patience in undoing the dropped stitches to make the ladders will be rewarded as you watch the garment go from darling to daring before your very eyes!

SIZES
XS (S, M)

Remember to use this guide to find your size based on your bust measurement: XS = 31"–33" (79cm–84cm); S = 34"–36" (86cm–91cm); M = 37"–39" (94cm–99cm).

KNITTED MEASUREMENTS
Bust: 32 (34, 36)" (81 [86, 91]cm)
Back length: 34½ (35¼, 35¼)" (87.5 [89.5, 89.5]cm)

MATERIALS
9 (10, 11) balls of Twinkle Handknits Kids Mohair, 40% wool/35% mohair/25% acrylic, 1¾ oz/50g, 310 yds/283m), #09 Black (2)

US size 15 (10mm) 24" (60cm) circular needle or size needed to obtain gauge

Crochet hook size E-4 (3.5mm)

Stitch holders

Stitch markers

Tapestry needle

GAUGE
10 stitches and 13 rows = 4" (10cm) in stockinette stitch (see page 150) with two strands held together on size 15 needle.

Take the time to check your gauge.

ABBREVIATIONS
C8L (cable 8 left): Slip next 4 stitches to cable needle and hold in front of work, k4, k4 from cable needle.
Dec 1 (decrease 1): At the beginning of a RS (WS) row, ssk (p2tog); at end of RS (WS) row, k2tog (ssp).
LadDec (ladder decrease): At the beginning of the row, work 1, then drop next (ladder) stitch from needle; continue across; at the end of the row, work to last 2 stitches, drop next (ladder) stitch from needle, then work 1.
Cable Pattern (8-stitch panel; see chart, page 56)
RNDS 1–4: K8.
RND 5: C8L.
RNDS 6–12: K8.
Repeat Rounds 1–12 for pattern.

NOTES

The tunic dress is knit in the round, then divided at the neck and worked back and forth, first in two, then in four sections. All sections are worked at the same time. Entire piece is worked with two strands held together throughout. Ladders are formed by casting on using backward loop and working stitches that are later intentionally dropped. Markers in three different colors should be used to indicate underarm, center front and back, and ladder stitches.

TUNIC

RNDS 1–2: ★K1, p1; repeat from ★ around.

RND 3 (ESTABLISH PATTERN): ★P1 (2, 1), k2 (2, 3), bind off next 3 stitches, work Rnd 1 of Cable Pattern (including stitch remaining from bind off), bind off next 6 stitches, k2 (2, 3), p1, slip underarm marker, p1 (2, 1), k2 (2, 3), bind off next 6 stitches, work Rnd 1 of Cable Pattern (including stitch remaining from bind off), bind off next 3 stitches, k2 (2, 3), p1, slip marker; repeat from ★ around—56 (60, 64) stitches.

RND 4: ★P1 (2, 1), k2 (2, 3), place ladder stitch marker, cast on 1 stitch over bound-off stitches using backward loop (ladder stitch), place ladder stitch marker, work Cable Pattern, place ladder stitch marker, cast on 2, place ladder stitch marker, k2 (2, 3), p1, slip marker, p1 (2, 1), k2 (2, 3), place ladder stitch marker, cast on 2, place ladder stitch marker, work Cable Pattern, place ladder stitch marker, cast on 1, place ladder stitch marker, k2 (2, 3), p1 (1, 1); repeat from ★ once—68 (72, 76) stitches.

Working ladder stitches in reverse stockinette stitch (purl every round), continue in established pattern until piece measures 20¾" (52.5cm) from beginning.

DIVIDE FOR NECK

ROW 1 (RS): Bind off 0 (1, 0), work in pattern to center Back marker, join new yarn and bind off 0 (1, 0), work to end—34 (35, 38) stitches remain for both Right Front/Back and Left Front/Back.

Working Right Front/Back and Left Front/Back at the same time with 2 separate balls of yarn, work 3 rows even.

SHAPE NECK

ROW 5 (RS): ★Dec 1, work in pattern to 2 stitches before center Back, dec1; continuing on Left Front/Back, repeat from ★ once—32 (33, 36) stitches remain on each side.

ROWS 6–7: Work even in pattern as established.

DIVIDE BODY

ROW 8 (WS): Work to 2 (1, 2) stitch(es) before left underarm marker, join new yarn and bind off next 4 (3, 4) stitches (removing marker), work across Left Back stitches; work to 2 (1, 2) stitch(es) before right underarm marker, join new yarn and bind off next 4 (3, 4) stitches (removing marker), work across Right Front stitches—14 (15, 16) stitches.

Work neck and armhole shaping on Fronts and Backs, placing decreases as indicated in Neck and Armhole Shaping Table on page 56 and working even on rows where cells are empty:

Work even until armhole measures 11¼ (12, 12)" (28.5 [30.5, 30.5]cm). Bind off.

FINISHING

Sew shoulder seams. Allow dropped stitches to ladder down to the corresponding cast-on stitch in Row 4.

With crochet hook and 2 strands held together, single crochet evenly around neck and armhole edges. Weave in ends.

NECK AND ARMHOLE SHAPING TABLE

	S	M	L
ROW 9			
ROW 10	LadDec at each armhole edge—13 stitches each section	Dec 1 at each underarm edge—14 stitches each section	Dec 1 at each armhole edge—15 stitches each section
ROW 11	Dec 1 at each neck edge—12 stitches	Dec 1 at each neck edge—13 stitches	Dec 1 at each neck edge—14 stitches
ROW 12			
ROW 13		LadDec at each armhole edge—12 stitches	LadDec at each armhole edge—13 stitches
ROW 14	LadDec at each armhole edge—11 stitches		
ROW 15			Dec 1 at each neck edge—12 stitches
ROW 16		LadDec at each armhole edge—11 stitches	LadDec at each armhole edge—11 stitches
ROW 17	LadDec at each neck edge—10 stitches	LadDec at each neck edge—10 stitches	LadDec at each neck edge—10 stitches

CABLE PATTERN CHART

Key

☐ K on RS, P on WS

⬭ C8L

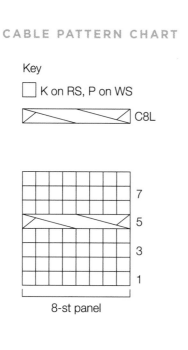

8-st panel

BELLE DU JOUR TUNIC SCHEMATIC

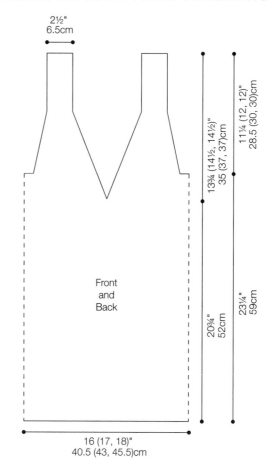

2½"
6.5cm

11¼ (12, 12)"
28.5 (30, 30)cm

13¾ (14½, 14½)"
35 (37, 37)cm

Front
and
Back

20¾"
52cm

23¼"
59cm

16 (17, 18)"
40.5 (43, 45.5)cm

metropolitan diary skirt

page 16

To make this feminine, eye-catching skirt, you'll knit a tube in the round that begins near the hem and narrows toward a ribbed waist. Then, pick up stitches along the hem edge to crochet the open loops that add a bit of shimmy to the Metropolitan Diary Skirt. The decrease lines accent the skirt's flared shape and detail the front with a crafty, handmade touch. The openness of the crocheted edge adds interest without a lot of weight. For proper fit, the dimensions of the finished waistline allow for the yarn's stretchiness by reflecting some negative ease.

SIZES
S (M, L)

Remember to use this guide to find your size based on your waist measurement: S = 28"–30" (71cm–76cm); M = 31"–32" (79cm–81cm); L = 33"–35" (84cm–89cm).

KNITTED MEASUREMENTS
Waist: 25$\frac{1}{2}$ (28, 30$\frac{1}{2}$)" (67.5 [71, 77.5]cm)

Length (including ruffle): 16$\frac{1}{4}$ (17$\frac{1}{4}$, 18$\frac{1}{4}$)" (41 [43.5, 46]cm)

MATERIALS
2 (2, 2) hanks Twinkle Handknits Soft Chunky, 100% virgin merino wool, 7 oz/200g, 83 yds/75m, #16 Carnation 🐨

US size 19 (15mm) 24" (60cm) and 29" (75cm) circular needles or size needed to obtain gauge

Size K-10$\frac{1}{2}$ (6.5 mm) crochet hook

Stitch markers

Tapestry needle

GAUGE
11 stitches and 16$\frac{1}{2}$ rows = 7" (18cm) in stockinette stitch (see page 150) on size 19 (15mm) needle.

Take the time to check your gauge.

ABBREVIATIONS
Bias Rnd: *Knit to marker, slip marker, M1-R, knit to 2 stitches before next marker, ssk, slip marker, k4, slip marker, k2tog, knit to next marker, M1-L, slip marker, repeat from * once, knit to end of round.

Dec Rnd: *Knit to marker, slip marker, M1-R, knit to 3 stitches before next marker, sssk, slip marker, k4, slip marker, k3tog, knit to next marker, M1-L, slip marker; rep from * once, knit to end of round. (Decreases 4 stitches each round.)

NOTES
The skirt is knit in the round. Mark the beginning of the round with a stitch marker in a different color from the others. Change to shorter needle when necessary.

SKIRT SHAPING TABLE

	Small	Medium	Large
RND 5	Bias Rnd	Dec Rnd	Bias Rnd
RND 9	Dec Rnd	Bias Rnd	Dec Rnd
RND 13	Bias Rnd	Dec Rnd	Bias Rnd
RND 17	Dec Rnd	Bias Rnd	Bias Rnd
RND 21	Bias Rnd	Dec Rnd	Dec Rnd
RND 23	Go to ribbing	Bias Rnd	Knit
RND 25	- -	Go to ribbing	Bias Rnd

SKIRT

With longer needle, and using cable cast-on, cast on 48 (56, 56) stitches, turn. Join, being careful not to twist stitches; place marker for beginning of round.

RND 1: *P6 (7, 7), place marker, p5, place marker, p4 center stitches, place marker, p5, place marker, p6 (7, 7), repeat from * once.

RNDS 2–22 (24, 26): Continuing in stockinette stitch (knit every round), work Bias Rnds and Dec Rnds according to Skirt Shaping Table— 40 (44, 48) stitches remain when all shaping is complete.

Change to k1, p1 rib (see page 150) and work even for 2 rounds. Bind off loosely in rib.

CROCHET EDGING

With right side facing and using crochet hook, join yarn to cast-on edge.

RND 1: Ch 1, sc in same stitch, *skip 2 cast-on stitches, 5 dc in next stitch, skip 2 cast-on stitches, sc in next stitch, ch 2, skip 2 cast-on stitches, sc in next stitch; repeat from * 3 (4, 4) times; end skip 3 (2, 2) cast-on stitches, 5 dc in next stitch, skip 3 cast-on stitches, sc in next stitch, ch 2, skip 3 cast-on stitches, sc in first ch to join.

RND 2: Ch 1, sc in previous sc, dc in next dc, (ch 1, dc in next dc) 4 times, sc in ch-2 space; repeat from * around, join with slip stitch to top of starting ch-1.

RND 3: Slip stitch in next dc, ch 5 (counts as dc and ch 2), (dc in next dc, ch 2) 3 times, dc in next dc, *(dc in next dc, ch 2) 4 times, dc in next dc; repeat from * around, join with slip stitch to 3rd ch of starting ch-5.

RND 4: Ch 1, 3 sc in ch-2 space, *ch 6, 3 sc in next ch-2 space; repeat from * around, ch 6, join with slip stitch to starting ch-1. Fasten off.

FINISHING

Weave in ends.

METROPOLITAN DIARY SKIRT SCHEMATIC

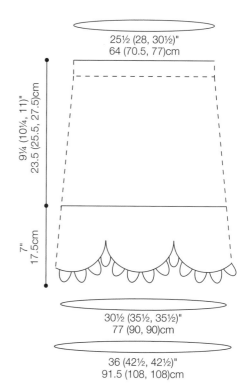

25½ (28, 30½)"
64 (70.5, 77)cm

9¼ (10¼, 11)"
23.5 (25.5, 27.5)cm

7"
17.5cm

30½ (35½, 35½)"
77 (90, 90)cm

36 (42½, 42½)"
91.5 (108, 108)cm

vauxhall poet's scarf

page 17

Scarves fashioned from chunky yarns are especially wearable when the pattern calls for openwork that delivers lightness and lessens bulk. Here, a simple (and two-sided) increase-and-decrease stitch pattern—the Purse Stitch—creates lengthwise stripes set beside regular columns of diagonally oriented twists. The end result looks almost like cut gems when rendered in Soft Chunky yarn in this rich color scheme. An orderly pattern, the Vauxhall Poet's Scarf features tidy borders of fringe that reinforce its traditional prep school properness. A straightforward pattern that requires few tools, this design is an easy travel companion and yields a perfect gift.

SIZE
One Size

KNITTED MEASUREMENTS
Approximately 8" x 70" (20.5cm x 178cm)

MATERIALS
3 hanks Twinkle Handknits Soft Chunky, 100% virgin merino wool, 7 oz/200g, 83 yds/75m, #01 Eggplant **6**

US size 17 (12.75mm) needles or size needed to obtain gauge

Large crochet hook (for attaching fringe)

Tapestry needle

GAUGE
14 stitches and 20 rows = 8¼" (21cm) in Purse Stitch Pattern on size 17 (12.75mm) needles.

Take the time to check your gauge.

Purse Stitch Pattern (multiple of 2 + 2)
ROW 1 (RS): K1, *yo, p2tog; repeat from * to last stitch, k1.
Repeat Row 1.

NOTE
The cast-on and bind-off must be done very loosely to accommodate the lateral stretch of the pattern stitch. Use two needles held together if necessary.

SCARF
Using cable cast-on, cast on 14 stitches very loosely.

Work in Purse Stitch Pattern for 170 rows, or approximately 70" (178cm).

Bind off very loosely.

Weave in ends.

FRINGE
Cut 28 strands of yarn, each 26" (66cm) long.

With crochet hook, attach 7 sets of double-stranded fringe to each end of scarf.

urban legend skirt

page 18

Trios of "knit 2 together" (k2tog) decreases—knitting two stitches together as if they were one—done successively and then followed by yarn overs creates the characteristic flirty openwork and wavy shape in the Urban Legend Skirt's knit pattern. The springy yarn provides the elastic, cozy grip at the waist needed to hold this skirt on your body and show off the skirt's shape. For that reason, you'll find small finished waistline measurements on the schematic.

SIZES
S (M, L)

Remember to use this guide to find your size based on your waist measurement: S = 28"–30" (71cm–76cm); M = 31"–32" (79cm–81cm); L = 33"–35" (84cm–89cm).

KNITTED MEASUREMENTS
Top circumference: 23 (25½, 28)" (58.5 [65, 71]cm)

Length: 39½" (100.5cm)

MATERIALS
4 (4, 4) hanks Twinkle Handknits Soft Chunky, 100% virgin merino wool, 7 oz/200g, 83 yds/75m, #04 Coral (A); 3 (3, 4) skeins, #06 Baby Pink (B) **6**

US size 19 (15mm) 24" (60cm) and 29" (75cm) circular needles or size needed to obtain gauge

Stitch marker

Tapestry needle

GAUGE
11 stitches and 16¼ rows = 7" (18cm) in Feather and Fan Stripe Pattern on size 19 (15mm) needles.

Take the time to check your gauge.

Feather and Fan Stripe Pattern (multiple of 18 + 0 (2, 4); see chart, page 61)
ROW 1 (RS): With A, knit.
ROW 2: Purl.
ROW 3: K0 (1, 2), *(k2tog) 3 times, (yo, k1) 6 times, (k2tog) 3 times; repeat from * twice, k0 (1, 2).
ROW 4: Knit.
ROWS 5–8: With B, repeat Rows 1–4.
Repeat Rows 1–8 for Feather and Fan Stripe Pattern.

NOTES
The skirt is knit back and forth in two pieces, then joined; the ribbing is worked in the round. A circular needle is used to accommodate the many stitches. Change yarn colors every four rows, carrying unused yarn loosely along the side of the fabric.

When decreasing at the sides of the Feather and Fan Stripe pattern, maintain proper stitch count by eliminating one yarn over for each k2tog that is eliminated in the pattern stitch. At the end of each patterned row following a decrease, count your stitches to make sure that you have compensated correctly. When you are finished with all shaping decreases, you will have eliminated two complete pattern repeats, one on each side.

SKIRT (MAKE 2 PIECES)

With longer needle and A, cast on 54 (56, 58) stitches.

ROWS 1–4: Work Feather and Fan Stripe Pattern.

ROW 5 (RS DEC ROW): With B, k2tog, knit to last 2 stitches, ssk—52 (54, 56) stitches.

ROW 6 (WS DEC ROW): Ssp, purl to last 2 stitches, p2tog—50 (52, 54) stitches.

ROW 7: Work Feather and Fan pattern row, eliminating yarn overs as necessary (see Notes). Count your stitches.

Continuing in established Feather and Fan Stripe Pattern, repeat RS Dec Rows and WS Dec Rows on the first two rows of each of the next 2 stripes—46 (48, 50) stitches remain after 3rd stripe and 42 (44, 46) stitches remain after 4th stripe.

Repeat RS Dec row on first row of each of the next 4 stripes—40 (42, 44) stitches remain after 5th stripe; 38 (40, 42) stitches remain after 6th stripe; 36 (38, 40) stitches remain after 7th stripe; 34 (36, 38) stitches remain after 8th stripe.

Continuing to decrease in this manner, eliminating a yarn over for each k2tog eliminated, ★decrease 1 stitch at each side of the first row of each of the next 2 stripes, then work 1 4-row stripe even; repeat from ★ 3 times—18 (20, 22) stitches. After 10th stripe in B is complete, cut B.

With A, work Rows 1–4 of Feather and Fan Stripe Pattern twice more.

Put stitches on holder and make second piece.

When second piece is complete, slip both pieces to shorter needle, join, and place marker to indicate beginning of round—36 (40, 44) stitches.

Work 4 rounds k1, p1 rib (see page 150).

Bind off loosely.

FINISHING

Sew side seams. Weave in ends.

FEATHER AND FAN STRIPE PATTERN CHART

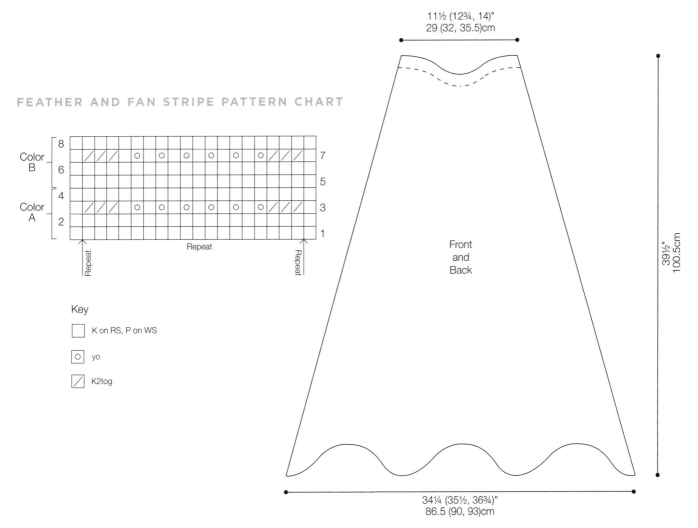

URBAN LEGEND SKIRT SCHEMATIC

weaver's cardigan

page 19

Reverse stockinette stitch gives this relaxed-fit, comfy cardi a bit of texture and creates the dashed-line border between the stripes of color. Garter stitch at the cuffs and bottom hem keep the edges from curling. The front panels are not shaped for the shoulder seam, allowing the shoulders to be seamed at the back for a sleek shoulder. This technique allows the bobbled stripe to climb up the princess line uninterrupted—a classic Twinkle construction method that contributes to this knit's refined silhouette.

SIZES

XS (S, M, L)

Remember to use this guide to find your size based on your bust measurement: XS = 31"–33" (79cm–84cm); S = 34"–36" (86cm–91cm); M = 37"–39" (94cm–99cm); L = 40"–42" (102cm–107cm).

KNITTED MEASUREMENTS

Bust (buttoned): 32½ (35¼, 38, 40¼)" (82.5 [89.5, 96.5, 102]cm)

Back length (not including neck band): 29 (29½, 30, 30½)" (74 [75, 76, 77.5]cm)

MATERIALS

3 (3, 3, 4) hanks Twinkle Handknits Soft Chunky, 100% virgin merino wool, 7 oz/200g, 83 yds/75m, #08 White (A); 2 skeins in #09 Black (B); 1 (1, 1, 2) skein(s) in #22 Sea Green (C); 1 skein in #12 Riviera (D) 🄶

US size 19 (15mm) 29" (75cm) circular needle or size needed to obtain gauge.

Stitch holders

Stitch markers

Tapestry needle

Nine 1⅝" (4cm) buttons

GAUGE

11 stitches and 16½ rows = 7" (18cm) in reverse stockinette stitch on size 19 (15mm) needles.

Take the time to check your gauge.

ABBREVIATIONS

Inc 1 (increase 1): Maintaining pattern, knit (or purl) 1 into right loop of stitch in row below next stitch on left-hand needle, then knit (or purl) the next stitch on left-hand needle.

MB (make bobble): (K1, p1, k1) into next stitch, turn; p3, turn; k3tog.

RS Dec Row: P2tog, purl to last 2 stitches, ssp.

WS Dec Row: Ssk, knit to last 2 stitches, k2tog.

RS Inc Row: P1, inc1, purl to last stitch, Inc 1, p1.

WS Inc Row: K1, inc1, knit to last stitch, Inc 1, k1.

Bobble Pattern (3-stitch panel; see chart, page 64)

ROW 1 AND ALL RS ROWS: P1, k1 tbl, p1.

ROW 2: K1, MB, k1.

ROWS 4 AND 6: K1, p1 tbl, k1.

ROW 8: MB, p1 tbl, MB.

ROWS 10 AND 12: Repeat Row 4.

Repeat Rows 1–12 for pattern.

Stripe Sequence

Including the cast-on row, work 6 rows each of B, C, A, D, B, C, then continue in A.

The sleeves and body are knit back and forth; a circular needle is used to accommodate the many stitches. The Bobble Pattern and Stripe Sequence are worked at the same time on the Body. The Back shoulders are shaped while the Front shoulders are not, thereby throwing the shoulder seam to the back.

BODY

With B, and using long-tail cast-on method, cast on 10 (11, 12, 13) stitches, place marker to indicate right underarm, cast on 26 (28, 30, 32) stitches, place marker to indicate left underarm, cast on 10 (11, 12, 13) stitches—46 (50, 54, 58) stitches.

Knit 3 rows, ending with a wrong-side row.

Change to reverse stockinette stitch (see page 150) and work 2 rows.

ESTABLISH PATTERNS (RS): With C, p4, work Row 1 of Bobble Pattern across next 3 stitches, purl to last 7 stitches, work Row 1 of Bobble Pattern across next 3 stitches, p4.

Work 7 rows even in established Stripe Sequence and Bobble Pattern, keeping remaining stitches in reverse stockinette stitch.

NEXT ROW (DEC ROW): Work to 3 stitches before marker, ssp, p1, slip marker, p1, p2tog; repeat from ★ once, work to end—42 (46, 50, 54) stitches.

Work 11 rows even, then repeat Dec Row—38 (42, 46, 50) stitches.

Work 5 rows even.

NEXT ROW (INC ROW): Work to 1 stitch before marker, inc 1, p1, slip marker,

p1, inc 1; repeat from ★ once, work to end—42 (46, 50, 54) stitches.

Work 11 rows even, then repeat Inc Row—46 (50, 54, 58) stitches.

Work even until Body measures 21" (53.5cm) from the beginning, ending with a wrong-side row.

DIVIDE BODY

NEXT ROW (RS): Removing markers, work to 2 stitches before marker, ssp, place these 9 (10, 11, 12) Right Front stitches on holder; p2tog, work to 2 stitches before next marker, ssp, place these 24 (26, 28, 30) Back stitches on holder; p2tog, work to end—9 (10, 11, 12) Left Front stitches.

LEFT FRONT

Work 1 row even.

NEXT ROW (RS): P2tog, work to end of row—8 (9, 10, 11) stitches.

Work 8 (10, 10, 12) rows even, ending with a right-side row.

NECK SHAPING

When beginning neck shaping, continue Bobble Pattern but omit the bobbles themselves. Bind off 2 stitches at the beginning of the next row and 1 stitch at the beginning of the following wrong-side row—5 (6, 7, 8) stitches.

Work 5 (4, 5, 4) rows even.

Bind off.

BACK

Place 24 (26, 28, 30) Back stitches onto needle. With wrong side facing, knit 1 row.

Work RS Dec Row (see Abbreviations, page 154) on next row and on following right-side row—

20 (22, 24, 26) stitches.

Work 9 (9, 10, 11) rows even.

Back Shoulder Shaping: Working RS Dec Rows or WS Dec Rows as appropriate, decrease 1 stitch at each side on next 5 (6, 6, 6) rows.

Slip remaining 10 (10, 12, 14) stitches to holder for Back Neck.

RIGHT FRONT

Place 9 (10, 11, 12) Right Front stitches onto needle. With wrong side facing, work 1 row.

NEXT ROW (RS): Work to last 2 stitches, ssp—8 (9, 10, 11) stitches.

Work 9 (11, 11, 13) rows even, ending with a wrong-side row.

NECK SHAPING

When beginning neck shaping, continue Bobble Pattern but omit the bobbles themselves. Bind off 2 stitches at the beginning of the next row and 1 stitch at the beginning of the following right-side row—5 (6, 7, 8) stitches.

Work 4 (3, 4, 3) rows even.

Bind off.

SLEEVES (MAKE 2)

With B, and using long-tail cast-on, cast on 17 stitches. Knit 3 rows, ending with a wrong-side row.

Change to reverse stockinette stitch and work 2 rows.

With C, continue Stripe Sequence as established.

SIZE M ONLY

Work 20 rows even. Work RS Inc Row—19 stitches.

SIZE L ONLY

Work 20 rows even. Work RS Inc Row—19 stitches. Work 9 rows even, then repeat RS Inc Row—21 stitches.

ALL SIZES

Work even until Sleeve measures 21"(53.5cm) from the beginning.

SLEEVE CAP

Working RS Dec Rows or WS Dec Rows as appropriate, dec 1 stitch at each side on the next row, then every 3 rows 0 (2, 2, 1) times, then every other row 4 (2, 2, 4) times—7 (7, 9, 9) stitches. Work even 1 (1, 1, 0) row. Bind off.

FINISHING

Sew front shoulders to shaped back shoulders.

NECK BAND

With right side facing and using A, pick up and knit 8 stitches along front neck edge, knit 10 (10, 12, 14) stitches from back neck holder, pick up and knit a 9 stitches along front neck edge—27 (27, 29, 31) stitches.

Work in k1, p1 rib for 2 rows. With B, work 2 rows in rib. With A, work 3 rows in rib. Bind off.

BUTTON BAND

With right side facing and using B, pick up and knit 62 stitches down Left Front edge, including side of Neck Band. Work 2 rows in k1, p1 rib. With A, work 2 rows in rib. With B, work 3 rows in rib. Bind off.

BUTTONHOLE BAND

With right side facing and using B, pick up and knit 62 stitches up Right Front edge, including side of Neck Band.

Work 2 rows in k1, p1 rib.

NEXT ROW (BUTTONHOLE ROW, WS): With A, work 2 stitches, ★yo, k2tog or p2tog as appropriate to maintain pattern, work 5 stitches; repeat from ★ to last 4 stitches, yo, k2tog or p2tog, work 2 stitches.

Work 1 row in rib.

With B, work 3 rows in rib. Bind off.

Pull bobbles to the right side if necessary. Sew in sleeves, easing in fullness around sleeve cap. Sew sleeve seams. Weave in ends. Sew on buttons, creating shanks if necessary to accommodate the thickness of the knit fabric.

WEAVER'S CARDIGAN BOBBLE CHART

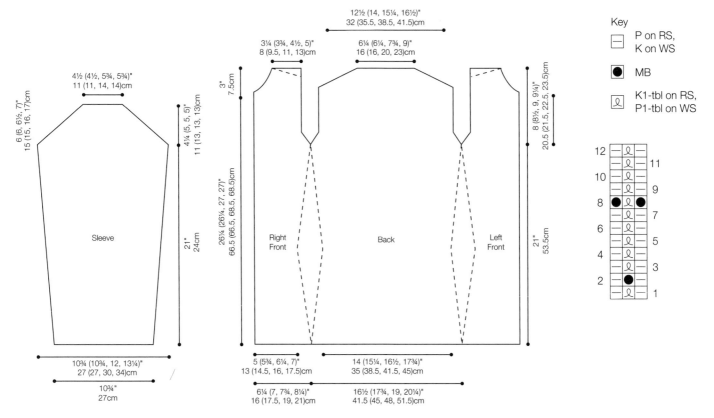

WEAVER'S CARDIGAN SCHEMATICS

Key

☐ P on RS, K on WS

⬤ MB

Ɋ K1-tbl on RS, P1-tbl on WS

Vacuum Packed: Big Knits in Small Spaces

Seasoned travelers know that packing a bag is a little like decorating a room: Make an initial selection of what to include and then edit out about a third of the items. Living spaces and suitcase alike need a little breathing space.

Lightening your travel load speeds passage through airports and hotel lobbies; narrowing your choices simplifies dressing, letting you focus on the day's fun. Twinkle tourists have the advantage of knowing that knits make great travel companions: They don't wrinkle like woven items, can be dressed up or down, and can be compressed into tight spaces in bags. Casual, layered looks are great for trips, too, when you're out of your room for hours and subject to a day's range of temperatures. Many of the designs in this book can do double duty for day or evening and be combined with other wardrobe staples you've packed.

Don't be put off by the bulk of chunky yarns when packing for travel or even home storage. Twinkle knits and yarns will surrender a good bit of real estate if you know how to handle them. The springiness that gives Twinkle yarns their volume and Twinkle knits their stretch and give is built on the wool's loosely spun and resilient structure: Collapse that structure with some pressure and you've gained valuable space; release the pressure and the yarn plumps up to regain its original shape. Packing knits in transparent, resealable bags that that can be compressed and then tightly closed is an easy way to do this. Items stored thusly are safe from moths and moisture and occupy a fraction of their usual volume. Pressing out the air also keeps contents from shifting during travel, preventing wrinkles. And when you're trying to close that smartly packed suitcase, the stacked bags can be easily shimmied into voids inside your bag or out of a zipper's teeth. I like oversized bags such as XL and XXL Ziplocs, which have double press-and-seal tops and gusseted bottoms to accommodate larger garments for travel. They also offer ample storage for yarn and garments at home. Put in a sachet filled with lavender, rosemary, or cedar chips to keep the contents smelling fresh and as a second-line defense against pest such as moths.

At some point, it's inevitable: You have to come home. If you've purchased souvenirs while on holiday, don't forget that breakables can be tucked in among knits for a cushioned ride. Be sure to place such knit-padded bags in the center of your suitcase and arrange shoes, cosmetic bags, cameras, or other dense, heavy items so they don't press against the breakables. Some travelers like to center fragile items in their bags surrounded by bolsters of rolled clothes or cushiony things that line the perimeter. Twenty skeins of pretty wool once served that purpose for me en route back from Paris. Perhaps a few Twinkle knits can do the same for you on your next holiday!

matinee coat

page 20

Part of the Twinkle charm lies in the exuberant play with proportions, textures, and scale. This pattern tinkers with all three. Pleats along one edge account for the generous volume of the sleeves. A semicircular, crochet-bordered band attached to the front edge creates the whimsical ruffle, and the shaped patch pockets further emphasize the coat's extravagant profile. Even the stitch pattern surprises: Reverse stockinette —the "wrong" side—is the public face. The rear-seamed shoulder creates a contoured, flattering décolleté. Intended to be layered over other garments, this coat fits more loosely than many Twinkle pieces.

SIZES

XS (S, M, L)

Remember to use this guide to find your size based on your bust measurement: XS = 31"–33" (79cm–84cm); S = 34"–36" (86cm–91cm); M = 37"–39" (94cm–99cm); L = 40"–42" (102cm–107cm).

KNITTED MEASUREMENTS

Bust (buttoned): $35^3/_4$ ($38^1/_4$, $40^3/_4$, $43^1/_4$)" (90.5 [97, 103, 109.5]cm)
Back length: $31^1/_2$" (79.5cm)

MATERIALS

4 (4, 5, 5) hanks Twinkle Handknits Soft Chunky, 100% virgin merino wool, 7 oz/200g, 83 yds/75m, #09 Black (A) and 3 skeins in #19 Cream (B) (6)

US size 17 (12.75mm) 29" (75cm) circular needle

US size 19 (15mm) 24" (60cm) circular needle or size needed to obtain gauge

3 US size 19 (15mm) double-pointed needles (for pleats)

US Size 7 (4.5mm) crochet hook

Stitch holders

6 stitch markers in three different colors

Tapestry needle

5 $1^5/_8$" (4cm) buttons

GAUGE

11 stitches and $16^1/_2$ rows = 7" (18cm) in reverse stockinette stitch on size 19 (15mm) needle.
Take the time to check your gauge.

ABBREVIATION

N1, N2, etc: Needle 1, needle 2, etc.

NOTES

A circular needle is used to accommodate the many stitches. The Fronts are worked without shoulder shaping, throwing the shoulder seam to the back. Sleeve cap pleats are formed on the bind-off row.

BODY

With larger needle and B, usng long-tail cast on, cast on 15 (16, 17, 18) Right Front stitches, place marker to indicate right underarm, cast on 32 (34, 36, 38) Back stitches, place marker to indicate left underarm, cast on 9 (10, 11, 12) Left Front stitches—56 (60, 64, 68) stitches.

Knit 3 rows (2 ridges).

Change to reverse stockinette stitch, beginning with a right-side row, and work 18 rows even. Cut B.

With A, work 4 rows reverse stockinette stitch.

Next Row (Buttonhole Row): P3, yo, p2tog, purl to end.

Continue in reverse stockinette stitch, working Buttonhole Row every 6 rows 4 times more, and at the same time, when Body measures 20" (51cm) from the beg, ending with a wrong-side row, divide body as follows.

DIVIDE BODY
NEXT ROW (RS): Removing markers, purl to 1 stitch before marker, place these 14 (15, 16, 17) Right Front stitches on holder, bind off 2 stitches, purl to 1 stitch before marker, place these 30 (32, 34, 36) Back stitches on holder, bind off 2 stitches, purl to end—8 (9, 10,11) Left Front stitches remain.

LEFT FRONT

Work 6 rows even. Place marker in front edge to indicate front band placement.

Work 20 rows even.

Bind off.

BACK

Place 30 (32, 34, 36) Back stitches on needle.

Beginning with wrong side facing, work 2 rows even.

NEXT ROW (DEC ROW)

Ssk, knit to last 2 stitches, k2tog—28 (30, 32, 34) stitches.

SIZES M AND L ONLY

Work 5 rows even, then repeat Dec row— 30 (32) stitches.

ALL SIZES

Work 13 (13, 7, 7) rows even.

SHAPE SHOULDERS
NEXT ROW (WS): Sssk, knit to last 3 stitches, k3tog—24 (26, 26, 28) stitches.

Purl 1 row.

Continue to decrease 2 stitches at each edge every wrong-side row 4 times more—8 (10, 10, 12) stitches remain. Bind off.

RIGHT FRONT

Place 14 (15, 16, 17) Right Front stitches on needle.

Beginning with wrong side facing, work 7 rows even, continuing Buttonhole Rows as established.

SHAPE NECK

Bind off 2 stitches at the beginning of the next 2 right-side rows, then bind off 1 stitch at the beginning of the following 2 right-side rows—8 (9, 10, 11) stitches.

Work even until Right Front measures same as Left Front. Bind off.

LEFT SLEEVE

With smaller needle and A, and using cable cast-on, cast on 25 (27, 27, 29) stitches.

ROW 1 (RS): P1, *k1, p1; repeat from * across.

Work 3 rows in k1, p1 rib as established.

Change to larger needle and reverse stockinette stitch.

Work 2 rows with B, then 2 rows with A.

NEXT ROW (INC ROW): With B, p1, inc1, purl to last 2 stitches, inc1, p1—27 (29, 29, 31) stitches. Knit 1 row.

Work 2 rows with A, then 2 rows with B. Cut B.

With A, work Inc Row, then work 2 rows even—29 (31, 31, 33) stitches.

MAKE PLEATS
NEXT ROW (WS): K9 (10, 10, 11), place marker, k1, place marker *k4, place marker, k1, place marker; repeat from * once, k9 (10, 10, 11) stitches.

PLEAT INC ROW (RS): *Purl to marker, M1-p, slip marker, p1, slip marker, M1-p; repeat from * 2 times, purl to end—35 (37, 37, 39) stitches.

Repeat Pleat Inc Row every other row 2 times more—47 (49, 49, 51) stitches.

PLEATED BIND-OFF ROW (WS): Bind off 11 (12, 12, 13) stitches—1 stitch remains on right-hand needle and 35 (36, 36, 37) stitches remain on left-hand needle; slip next 2 stitches to one dpn and hold in front [N1], slip next 2 stitches to another dpn [N2], pivot N2 clockwise so that wrong side is facing and hold behind N1; slip next 5 stitches to another dpn [N3] and hold behind N2; holding N1, N2, and N3 parallel to and in front of the left-hand needle [N4], knit together next stitch from N1 and N3, bind off 1 stitch; knit together next stitch from N1, N2, and N3, bind off 1 stitch—0 stitches remain on N1, 1 stitch remains on N2, 3 stitches remain on N3; knit together next stitch from N2 and N3, bind off 1 stitch—2 stitches remain on N3; slip next 2 stitches from N4 to free dpn [N5], pivot N5 clockwise and hold behind N3; slip next 5 stitches from N4 to another dpn [N6] and hold behind N5; knit together next stitch from N3 and N6, bind off 1 stitch—1 stitch remains on N3, 4 stitches remain on N6; knit together next stitch from N3, N5, and N6, bind off 1 stitch—0 stitches remain on N3, 1 stitch remains on N5, 3 stitches remain on N6; knit together next stitch from N5 and N6, bind off 1 stitch—0 stitches remain on N5, 2 stitches remain on N6; slip next 2 stitches from N4 onto free dpn [N7], pivot N7 clockwise and hold behind N6; knit together next stitch from N6 and N4, bind off 1 stitch—1 stitch remains on N6; knit together next stitch from N6, N7, and N4, bind off 1 stitch—0 stitches remain on N6, 1 stitch remains on N7; knit together next stitch from N7 and N4, bind off 1 stitch—0 stitches remain on N7; bind off stitches to end.

RIGHT SLEEVE
Work as for Left Sleeve to Bind-Off Row.

PLEATED BIND-OFF ROW: Bind off 11 (12, 12, 13) stitches [1 stitch on right-hand needle and 35 (36, 36, 37) stitches remain on left-hand needle]; slip next 2 stitches to one dpn and hold in back [N1], slip next 2 stitches to another dpn [N2], pivot N2 counter-clockwise

so that wrong side is facing and hold in front of N1; slip next 5 stitches to another dpn [N3] and hold in front of N2; holding N3, N2, and N1 parallel to and behind left needle [N4], knit together next stitch from N3 and N1, bind off 1 stitch; knit together next stitch from N3, N2, and N1, bind off 1 stitch—3 stitches remain on N3, 1 stitch remains on N2, 0 stitches remain on N1; knit together next stitch from N3 and N2, bind off 1 stitch—2 stitches remain on N3; slip next 2 stitches from N4 to free dpn [N5], pivot counter-clockwise and hold in front of N3; slip next 5 stitches from N4 to another dpn [N6] and hold in front of N5; knit together next stitch from N6 and N3, bind off 1 stitch; knit together next stitch from N6, N5, and N3, bind off 1 stitch—0 stitches remain on N3, 1 stitch remains on N5, 3 stitches remain on N6; knit together next stitch from N6 and N5, bind off 1 stitch—2 stitches remain on N6; slip next 2 stitches from N4 onto free dpn [N7], pivot counter-clockwise and hold in front of N6; knit together next stitch from N4 and N6, bind off 1 stitch; knit together next stitch from N4, N7 and N6, bind off 1 stitch—0 stitches remain on N6, 1 stitch remains on N7; knit together next stitch from N4 and N7, bind off 1 stitch—0 stitches remain on N7; bind off stitches to end.

FINISHING
RUFFLE
With larger needle and B, and using long-tail cast-on, cast on 12 stitches.

ROW 1 (WS): Knit.
ROW 2: P8, wrap and turn (see Short Rows page 152).
ROW 3: Slip 1, k7.
ROW 4: P4, wrap and turn.
ROW 5: Slip 1, k3.

ROW 6: P12, picking up all wraps.

Repeat Rows 1–6 5 times more. Cut B.

Change to A and repeat Rows 1–6 12 times.

Work 2 rows reverse stockinette stitch. Bind off.

POCKETS (MAKE 2)
With larger needle and B, and using cable cast-on, cast on 10 stitches.

Working in reverse stockinette stitch, cast on 3 stitches at the end of the next 2 rows, then 2 stitches at the end of the following 2 rows—20 stitches.

Work 11 rows even.

Change to A and work 4 rows.

NEXT ROW (RS): P1, (p2tog) 9 times, p1—11 stitches.

Work 4 rows in k1, p1 rib (see page 150). Bind off.

LEFT FRONT BAND
With right side facing and using smaller needle, pick up 46 stitches from marker to lower edge, picking up approximately 4 stitches out of every 5 rows along the edge.

ROW 1 (WS): P2, ★k2, p2; repeat from ★ to end.

Work 3 more rows in established k2, p2 rib. Bind off.

Sew Fronts to Back shoulders, stretching as necessary to fit.

Sew shorter edge of Ruffle to Right Front edge, stretching as necessary to fit.

With right side facing and using crochet hook and B, single crochet 54 stitches across top edge of Ruffle, around neck edge and across top of Left Front band. Ch 1, turn, slip stitch in each stitch to end of row. Fasten off.

Sew in sleeves, easing in pleats across top of armhole. Sew sleeve seams.

Sew pockets centered below underarms with bottom just above garter stitch band, matching colors and forming a "rounded pouch" (see photo) as follows: Sew 10 cast on stitches of pocket across 10 stitches of coat. Sew sides of pockets directly above these 10 sts, forcing the pocket to "pouch out."

Weave in ends. Sew on buttons, creating shanks if necessary to accommodate the thickness of the knit fabric.

Twinkle Knit Bit

When working on an assembled garment, start with small pieces such as sleeves to help build confidence using unfamiliar needles, yarns, or patterns. Those items also serve well to check your gauge or stitch pattern. With small pieces, if you need to rework sections because your tension is too loose, for example, you'll have fewer stitches to take out than had you begun with a front or back of a sweater.

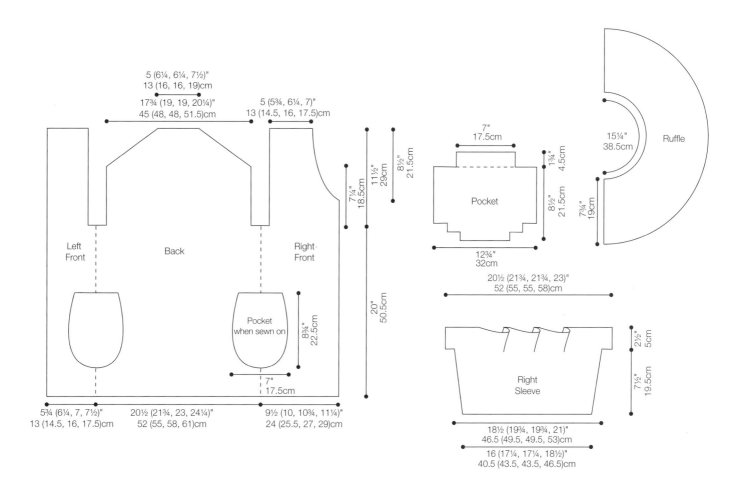

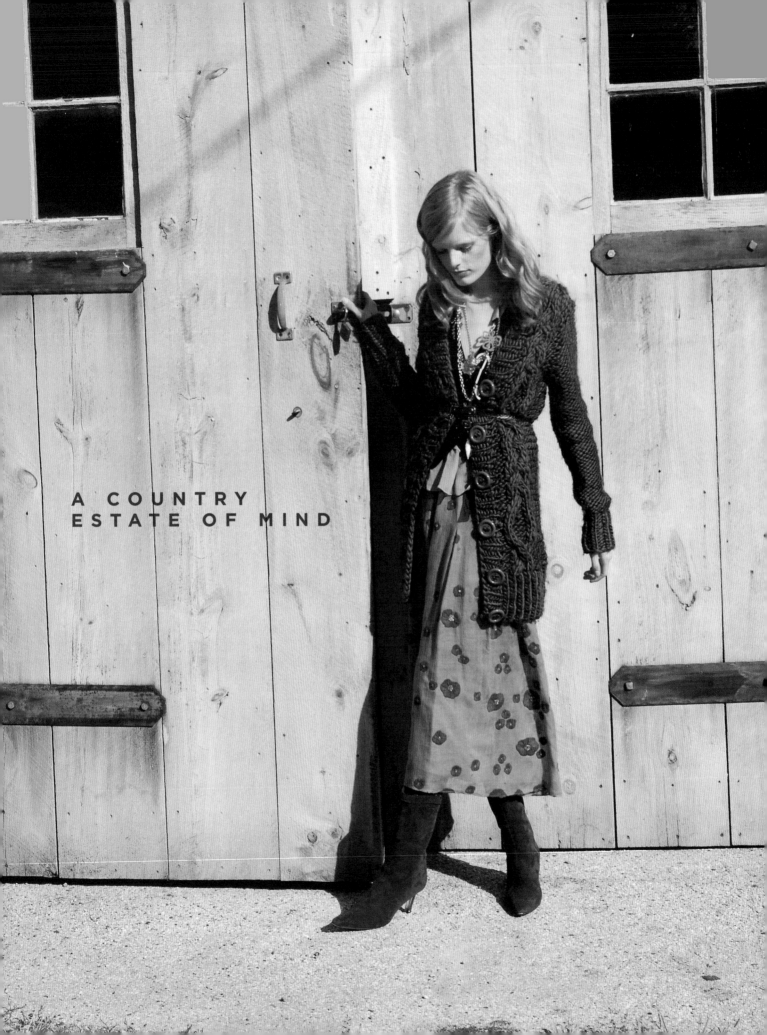

A COUNTRY
ESTATE OF MIND

PDA 4 PDA: Using the Internet for a Romantic Twinkle Trip

Internet research isn't just for perusing knitting websites. Savvy travelers bring their web-enabled PDAs or laptops to scout romantic restaurants, cozy inns, and chic nightclubs, as well as to map out a stroll to a scenic spot for a little public display of affection. Even while you're away from home, booking tickets for concerts, tours, and theater is often easier—and more economical—when done online with a credit card at your convenience and when exchange rates may be favorable.

Wi-Fi hotspots abound abroad, enabling you to connect to the Internet easily while on holiday. Bookmark these websites to find nearby Wi-Fi hotspots wherever you roam: www.jiwire.com and www.WiFinder.com.

Websites that post cultural calendars can help you plan itineraries. Visit sites like *Time Out* (www.timeout.com) and select the "city guides" tab to learn about art openings, concerts, and festivals scheduled during your holiday. Online forums where travelers rank and review travel destinations provide feedback and suggestions for hotels, restaurants, and attractions. Visit Chowhound (www.chowhound.com), for instance, to read posts by passionate and well-traveled food fans who weigh in on their favorite restaurants around the world.

A note to Twinkle travelers who haven't yet left home: Try some of my favorite websites, shown below, for planning your next glam getaway.

www.homeandabroad.com

Build a custom itinerary, based on trip length and interests, for about a hundred destinations. Or pick from itineraries already created, including ones with themes such as family travel or romantic getaways. You can add comprehensive, indexed data about local attractions to your trip plan, as well as link to other websites supplying additional details.

www.concierge.com

This site culls articles from its host's travel magazine, *Condé Nast Traveler,* as well as provides content unique to the site. You'll find in-depth information about destinations, travel activities, and general tips. Use it in conjunction with homeandabroad.com.

www.sidestep.com

Featuring a useful grid to compare domestic and international airfares by carrier and number of stops, this one-stop site collects flight information from hundreds of airlines and websites (as well as data on hotels, car rentals, cruises, daytrips, and services). Click on its "Travel Guides" tab for general tourist info.

www.farecompare.com

Use this site to shop for international flights among most US carriers **and** many non-US-based ones. The site maintains a database of fare data from the past two years to help gauge a good fare and time to buy.

www.kayak.com

Like the above two sites, this is a clearinghouse of travel data of all kinds (and includes discount airlines like JetBlue) but its hotel information excels. It boasts an impressive number of listings, some drawn from customer reviews, and powerful search criteria.

www.tripadvisor.com

This heavily visited site offers copious—and well-regarded—customer reviews of lodging all around the world, as well as hotel- and flight-booking tools, travel forums, and plentiful general travel resources such as maps and lists of tourist attractions.

www.lastminute.com

Have a sudden urge to jet off with a beau to Zurich or Cape Cod? This site specializes in last-minute packages of flights and lodging (up to about two weeks in advance). You can also book special themed "experiences" (most of which include travel)—such as moonlight sailboat trips, paragliding outings, or dance lessons—for anniversaries, parties, or in selected destinations.

www.venere.com

Specializing in Italian accommodations, this cleanly-designed site books hotels, B&Bs, and flats in the US, UK, Austria, France, Germany, Greece, Italy, Portugal, Spain, Switzerland, and many other countries. Easy to navigate, it permits sorting choices by price, popularity, ratings, or name of hotel, and supplies many photos.

www.autoeurope.com

As its name suggests, this site offers discounted car rentals in Europe. It also rents scooters and cellphones. Call the 24-hour customer-service hotline (1-888-223-5555).

www.travelcell.com

For about $30/week, rent cellphones configured for use in nearly 150 countries, with free incoming local calls in more than 70 nations. TravelCell even lets you retain your stateside cellphone number for use abroad. Satellite phones connect you from remote areas.

new haven hat

page 24

This pattern is simple to work on double-pointed needles, shaped with simple decreases, and detailed with simple cables. Your efforts are rewarded with a simply indispensable hat that makes a great gift or addition to your own wardrobe. Front-crossed cables stand out against the purl-stitch background, encircling the hat and rising to meet at the crown. An attached band of the same cable pattern rings the brim, adding another three-dimensional detail. Seam it loosely so that it can stretch for a comfortable fit.

SIZE
One Size

KNITTED MEASUREMENTS
Circumference: 22$^1/_2$″ (57cm)
Depth: 9$^1/_2$″ (24cm) (including band)

MATERIALS
1 hank Twinkle Handknits Soft Chunky, 100% virgin merino wool, 7 oz/200g, 83 yds/75m, #04 Coral 6

One set of four or five US size 19 (15mm) double-pointed needles or size needed to obtain gauge

Cable needle

Tapestry needle

GAUGE
8 stitches and 8$^1/_2$ rounds = 4″ (10cm) over cable pattern on size 19 (15mm) needles.

Take the time to check your gauge.

ABBREVIATION
C4L (cable 4 left): Slip 2 stitches to cable needle and hold in front, k2, k2 from cable needle.

NOTES
This hat is knit in the round. The band is knit flat, then sewn onto lower edge of the hat.

HAT

Cast on 40 stitches. Divide evenly onto three or four double-pointed needles. Place marker and join, being careful not to twist stitches.

RNDS 1 AND 2: ★K4, p4; repeat from ★ around.
RND 3: ★C4L, p4; repeat from ★ around.
RND 4: Repeat Rnd 1.
RND 5: ★K4, p2, p2tog; repeat from ★ around—35 stitches.
RND 6: ★K4, p3; repeat from ★ around.
RND 7: ★C4L, p3; repeat from ★ around.
RND 8: Repeat Rnd 6.
RND 9: ★K4, p2tog, p1; repeat from ★ around—30 stitches.
RND 10: ★K4, p2; repeat from ★ around.
RND 11: ★C4L, p2; repeat from ★ around.
RND 12: Repeat Rnd 10.
RND 13: ★K4, p2tog; repeat from ★ around—25 stitches.
RND 14: ★K4, p1; repeat from ★ around.
RND 15: ★C4L, p1; repeat from ★ around.
RND 16: Repeat Rnd 14.

Cut yarn, leaving a 10" tail. Thread tail (250.5cm) through remaining 25 stitches, pull tight, and secure to wrong side.

BAND

Working back and forth on two double-pointed needles, and using cable cast-on, cast on 6 stitches.

ROW 1 (RS): P1, k4, p1.
ROW 2: K1, p4, k1.
ROW 3: P1, C4L, p1.
ROW 4: Repeat Row 2.

Repeat these 4 rows 11 times more. Bind off.

FINISHING

Sew cast-on edge to bound-off edge of band. Sew side edge of band around lower edge of hat.

Weave in ends.

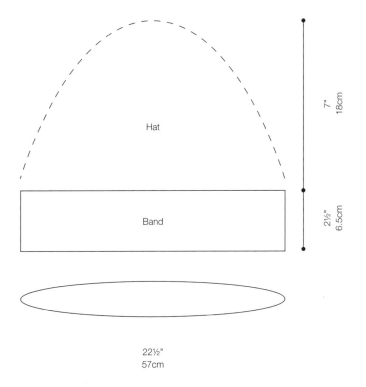

Hat

Band

7"
18cm

2½"
6.5cm

22½"
57cm

Twinkle Knit Bit

Like a lost mitten, a point protector gone AWOL leaves you stranded. Use a strand of yarn to connect a pair of point protectors in the way that children's mittens are tethered and you're stranded in a good way. Thread a darning or embroidery needle with a length of brightly colored yarn long enough to span the distance between the two needles' ends when your knitting is at rest. Carefully pierce both protectors, situating one at either end of the yarn. Knot each end of the yarn to anchor a protector at an end. You'll find that when attached to each other, the protectors are much easier to track down. Big projects made with heavy yarns can easily dislodge a typical protector, sending stitches careening off the needles. For such projects, make your own protectors from a pair of inexpensive rubber balls (miniature tennis balls from a pet store work well) pierced through one side with an awl or ice pick. The hole should be a little smaller than the diameter of your needle. Capping the ends of your big needles, the balls stay put yet are easy to remove, won't scratch or snag your work, and are big enough to keep stitches from slipping off.

middlebury scarf

page 24

Laid flat, the Middlebury Scarf is a spiral of repeated short-row wedges knitted in stockinette. When held along the short edge, however, it flutters in serpentine form. A crocheted picot trim, made by picking up stitches along the outer edge of the scarf, gives this accessory a delicate, vintage feel. The double-strand mohair construction is dense enough to supply a burst of color yet still be nearly weightless despite its generous length.

SIZE
One Size

KNITTED MEASUREMENTS
Approximately 8¹/₂ x 69¹/₂" (21.5cm x 176cm)

MATERIALS
2 balls of Twinkle Handknits Kids Mohair, 40% wool/35% mohair/25% acrylic, 1³/₄ oz/50g, 310 yds/283m), #19 Cream **2**

US size 15 (10mm) needles or size needed to obtain gauge

US size E-4 (3.5mm) crochet hook

Tapestry needle

GAUGE
10 stitches and 12 rows = 4" (10cm) in stockinette stitch with two strands held together on size 15 needles.

Take the time to check your gauge.

NOTES
The piece is worked in stockinette stitch with two strands held together. The scarf is shaped using short rows.

SCARF

With 2 strands held together, and using long-tail cast-on, cast on 21 stitches.

ROW 1 (WS): Purl.
ROW 2: K14, wrap and turn (see page 000).
ROW 3: P14.
ROW 4: K7, wrap and turn.
ROW 5: P7.

ROW 6: Knit across all stitches, picking up both wraps (see page 151).

Repeat Rows 1–6 until the shorter edge (the inner spiral length; see schematic) measures approximately 69" (175cm), ending with Row 6.

Bind off loosely.

EDGING

With right side facing and using crochet hook and 2 strands held together, join yarn in corner of longer edge. Ch 4, sc in same stitch as joining, ★sc in next stitch, ch 3, sc in same stitch; repeat from ★ to end, working along longer edge to corner. Fasten off.

Weave in ends.

MIDDLEBURY SCARF SCHEMATIC

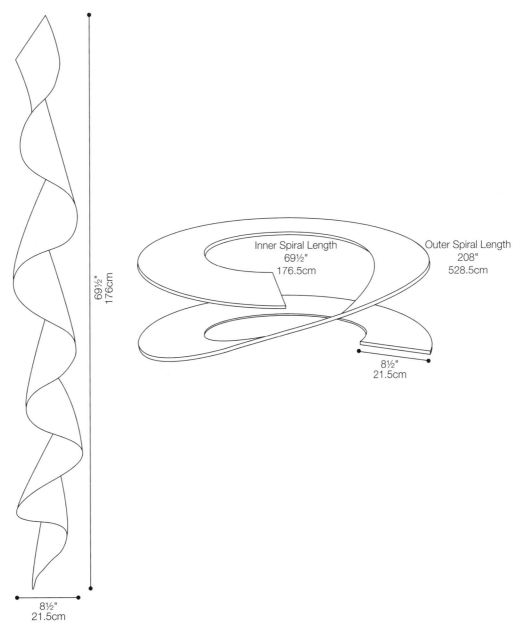

69½"
176cm

8½"
21.5cm

Inner Spiral Length
69½"
176.5cm

Outer Spiral Length
208"
528.5cm

8½"
21.5cm

bar harbor hoodie vest

page 26

Perennial Twinkle details abound in this eye-catching knit: subtle texture, shaped silhouette, amusing sleeves and hood, and clever construction. The seed stitch fabric envelops you in a cushiony layer, and a few decreases subtly draw in the waist before increases flare it out a bit toward the underarms. The hood is a continuation of a panel of the neck section whose sides are joined later. The pockets are knit as separate pieces, but pulling together the cast-on edges as they're sewn to the body gives them an endearing, pouch-like shape.

SIZES

XS (S, M, L)

Remember to use this guide to find your size based on your bust measurement: XS = 31"–33" (79cm–84cm); S = 34"–36" (86cm–91cm); M = 37"–39" (94cm–99cm); L = 40"–42" (102cm–107cm).

KNITTED MEASUREMENTS

Bust (buttoned): 29 (31¼, 33¾, 36)" (74 [79, 85.5, 91]cm)

Back length (not including hood): 27¼" (69cm)

MATERIALS

6 (7, 7, 8) hanks Twinkle Handknits Soft Chunky, 100% virgin merino wool, 7 oz/200g, 83 yds/75m, #14 Sapphire ⑥

US size 17 (12.75mm) 29" (75cm) circular needle

US size 19 (15mm) 29" (75cm) circular needle or size needed to obtain gauge.

Stitch holders

Stitch markers

Tapestry needle

Nine 1⅝" (4cm) buttons

GAUGE

10 stitches and 17 rows = 6" (15cm) in seed stitch on size 19 (15mm) needles.

Take the time to check your gauge.

ABBREVIATION

Dec 1 (decrease 1): K2tog when the second stitch to be decreased is a knit stitch; p2tog when the second stitch to be decreased is a purl stitch.

Seed Stitch Pattern (multiple of 2)
ROW 1 (RS): *K1, p1; repeat from * across.
ROW 2: Purl the knit stitches and knit the purl stitches.
Repeat Row 2 for pattern.

NOTES

A circular needle is used to accommodate the many stitches. First, the sleeves are worked back and forth, then the body is worked back and forth to the underarms. At that point, the sleeves are joined to the body and the sweater is worked in one piece. Work all increases maintaining Seed Stitch Pattern. The front neck drop is formed by working short rows. These short rows are counted like full rows when you are determining where to make decreases for raglan shaping. Use markers of different colors to indicate raglan shaping and sleeve shaping.

SLEEVES (MAKE 2)

With larger needle, and using cable cast-on, cast on 4 stitches, place marker to indicate center of Sleeve, cable cast on 4 stitches.

Begin Seed Stitch Pattern and work 2 rows.

Maintaining pattern, cast on 3 (4, 4, 4) stitches at the beginning of the next 2 rows, 3 stitches at the beginning of the following 2 rows, 1 stitch at the beginning of the following 2 rows, and 2 stitches at the beginning of the following 2 rows—26 (28, 28, 28) stitches. Place stitches on holder.

BODY

With smaller needle, cable cast on 10 (11, 12, 13) stitches, place marker to indicate right underarm, cable cast on 28 (30, 32, 34) stitches, place marker to indicate left underarm, cable cast on 10 (11, 12, 13) stitches—48 (52, 56, 60) stitches.

Work 8 rows in k2, p2 rib.

Change to the larger needle and work 16 rows even in Seed Stitch Pattern.

NEXT ROW (DEC ROW): *Work to 2 stitches before marker, dec 1, slip marker, dec 1; repeat from *, work to end—44 (48, 52, 56) stitches.

Repeat Dec Row every 6 rows twice more—36 (40, 44, 48) stitches. Work 5 rows even.

NEXT ROW (INC ROW): *Work to marker, inc 1, slip marker, inc 1; repeat from *, work to end—40 (44, 48, 52) stitches.

Work 3 rows even, then repeat Inc Row—44 (48, 52, 56) stitches.

Work even until Body measures approximately 17½" (44.5cm) from the beginning, ending with a wrong-side row.

DIVIDE BODY

ROW 1 (RS): *Work to 2 stitches before marker, bind off 4 stitches (removing marker); repeat from * once more, work to end.

JOIN BODY AND SLEEVES

ROW 2: Work 7 (8, 9, 10) Left Front stitches, place marker to indicate raglan shaping, work 26 (28, 28, 28) Left Sleeve stitches, place marker to indicate raglan shaping, work 22 (24, 26, 28) Back stitches, place marker to indicate raglan shaping, work 26 (28, 28, 28) Right Sleeve stitches, place marker to indicate raglan shaping, work 7 (8, 9, 10) Right Front stitches—88 (96, 100, 104) stitches.

NECK AND RAGLAN SHAPING

NOTE: READ ALL SHAPING INSTRUCTIONS BEFORE BEGINNING.

To decrease at center of sleeve [Center/Sleeve]: Work to 2 stitches before center Sleeve marker, dec 1, slip marker, dec 1.

To decrease before the raglan shaping marker: Work to 2 stitches before marker, dec 1.

To decrease following the raglan shaping marker: Slip marker, dec 1.

Work raglan shaping on Fronts, Back, and Sleeves, and shaping at Center/Sleeve markers, placing decreases as indicated in the Neck and Raglan Shaping Table on page 78 and working even on rows where cells are empty.

AT THE SAME TIME, on row marked ★★, work short rows as follows, maintaining raglan shaping:

Work to 3 stitches from Left Front edge, wrap and turn (see Short Rows on page 152); work to 3 stitches from Right Front edge, wrap and turn; work to 6 stitches from Left Front edge, wrap and turn; work to 6 stitches from Right Front edge, wrap and turn. Continue on all stitches, picking up all wraps (see page 151).

All sizes: 32 stitches remain when all shaping is complete.

HOOD

Work 24 rows even; on last row, place marker after first 16 stitches.

Dec 1 each side of marker on next row, then every other row 7 times—16 stitches. Place first 8 stitches on smaller needle and, using larger needle and holding stitches parallel, work three-needle bind-off (see page 153) across all stitches.

FRONT BAND

With right side facing and using smaller needle, beginning at lower Right Front, pick up and knit 57 stitches along Right Front edge, 62 stitches along Hood and 57 stitches along Left Front edge—176 stitches.

ROW 1 (WS): P3, *k2, p2; repeat from *, ending last repeat with p3.
ROW 2 (BUTTONHOLE ROW): K3, *p2, k2, yo, p2tog; k2; repeat from * 6 times, continue in rib to end.

Work 3 more rows in rib as established.

Loosely bind off purlwise on wrong side.

NECK AND RAGLAN SHAPING TABLE

	XS	S	M	L
ROW 3				
ROW 4	Center/Sleeve	Center/Sleeve	Center/Sleeve	
ROW 5	Fronts, Back	Fronts, Back	Fronts, Back	Fronts, Back
ROW 6				Center/Sleeve
ROW 7				
ROW 8			Back	Fronts, Back
ROW 9	Center/Sleeve	Center/Sleeve	Center/Sleeve	
ROW 10		Fronts, Back	Fronts	
ROW 11				
ROW 12	Back		Back	Fronts, Back Center/Sleeve
ROW 13				
ROW 14	Center/Sleeve	Center/Sleeve	Center/Sleeve	
ROW 15	Fronts	Back	Fronts	
ROW 16		Fronts	Back	Fronts, Back
ROW 17				
ROW 18	Back			Center/Sleeve
ROW 19	Center/Sleeve	Center/Sleeve	Fronts, Center/Sleeve	Fronts, Back
ROW 20		Back	Back	
ROW 21				
ROW 22	Fronts	Fronts	Fronts	Fronts, Back
ROW 23**	Back			
ROW 24	Center/Sleeve	Center/Sleeve	Back, and Center/Sleeve	Center/Sleeve
ROW 25		Back		Back
ROW 26				
ROW 27				
ROW 28	Back, and Center/Sleeve	Back and Center/Sleeve	Back	Back

POCKETS (MAKE 2)

Leaving a 15" (38cm) tail and using larger needle, cable cast on 10 stitches.

Begin Seed Stitch Pattern and work 1 row.

Cast on 3 stitches at the beginning of the next 2 rows, and 2 stitches at the beginning of the following 2 rows—20 stitches.

Work 20 rows even.

Change to smaller needles and k2tog across—10 stitches.

Work 4 rows in k2, p2 rib. Bind off.

Thread yarn tail through all cast-on stitches and gather slightly. Place pocket just above ribbing, centered at underarm. Beginning with sides of pocket, sew into place, adjusting shirring as needed.

FINISHING

Turn up sleeve and sew button through both layers of fabric, using photo as a guide. Weave in ends. Sew on buttons, creating shanks if necessary to accommodate the thickness of the knit fabric

BAR HARBOR HOODIE VEST SCHEMATIC

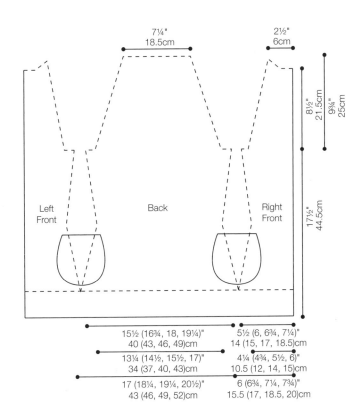

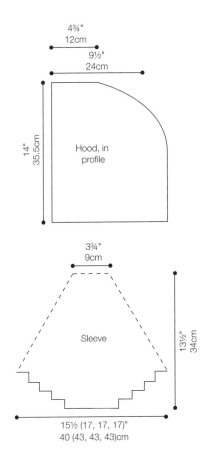

bookbrowser's sweater

page 27

The Bookbrowser's bobbled, raised-line motif evokes a budding hollyhock and is a tender touch that rises from the sweater's purled front. The purl bumps in the body of the sweater hide those places where stitches are picked up on the sleeves and shaped into shoulders by knitting in the round. The resulting silhouette is smooth and fitted and, to those used to set-in sleeves and seamed shoulders, appears almost magically formed to the body. Don't be worried about the negative ease; the yarn's stretchiness gives this sleek, fetching pullover a cozy snugness. As you build the folded split-neck turtleneck, picking up some stitches from the collar's inside edge allows you to create an elegant overlap at the split.

SIZES
S (M, L)

Remember to use this guide to find your size based on your bust measurement: XS = 31"–33" (79cm–84cm); S = 34"–36" (86cm–91cm); M = 37"–39" (94cm–99cm); L = 40"–42" (102cm–107cm).

KNITTED MEASUREMENTS
Bust: 27¼ (30, 32½)" (69 [76, 82.5]cm)

Back length (not including collar): 23¾ (24½, 25½)" (60 [62, 64.5]cm)

MATERIALS
4 (5, 5) hanks Twinkle Handknits Soft Chunky, 100% virgin merino wool, 7 oz/200g, 83 yds/75m, #05 Pink

US size 17 (12.75mm) 24" (60cm) circular needle

US size 19 (15mm) 29" (75cm) and 24" (60cm) circular needles or size needed to obtain gauge

Stitch holders

Stitch markers

Cable needle

Tapestry needle

One 1½" button

GAUGE
11 stitches and 16½ rows = 7" (18cm) in reverse stockinette stitch on size 19 (15mm) needles.

Take the time to check your gauge.

ABBREVIATIONS
Inc 1 (increase 1): Maintaining pattern, knit (or purl) 1 into right loop of stitch in row below next stitch on left-hand needle, then knit (or purl) the next stitch on left-hand needle.

MB (make bobble): (K1, p1, k1) into next stitch, turn; p3, turn; k3tog.

T2R (twist 2 right): Slip next stitch to cable needle and hold in back, k1, p1 from cable needle.

T2L (twist 2 left): Slip next stitch to cable needle and hold in front, p1, k1 from cable needle.

Bobble Vine Stitch Pattern (9-stitch panel; see chart, page 82)

RNDS 1–2: P3, k3, p3.
RND 3: P2, T2R, k1, T2L, p2.
RND 4: P2, (k1, p1) 3 times, p1.
RND 5: P1, T2R, p1, k1, p1, T2L, p1.
RND 6: P1, k1, (p2, k1) 2 times, p1.
RND 7: P1, MB, p1, k3, p1, MB, p1.
RND 8: Repeat Rnd 1.
Repeat Rnds 1–8 for pattern.

First, the sleeves are worked back and forth on a circular needle, then the body is worked in the round. The sleeves are joined to the body at the underarm and the sweater is knit in one piece from that point; change to a shorter circular needle when it is comfortable to do so. The front neck drop is formed by short rows; these short rows are counted like full rows when you are determining where to make decreases for raglan shaping. The collar is worked back and forth. Mark the beginning of the round with a stitch marker in a different color from the others.

SLEEVES (MAKE 2)

With smaller needle, and using cable cast-on, cast on 13 (15, 17) stitches.

ROW 1 (RS): K1, ★p1, k1; repeat from ★ across.

Continue in established rib for 11 more rows.

Change to larger needle and reverse stockinette stitch (see page 150).

NEXT ROW (INC ROW): P1, inc 1, purl to last 2 stitches, inc1, p1—15 (17, 19) stitches.

Work 13 rows, then repeat Inc Row—17 (19, 21) stitches.

Work even until Sleeve measures 16" (40.5cm) from the beginning, ending with a wrong-side row.

UNDERARM SHAPING

Bind off 2 stitches at the beginning of the next row and 1 stitch at the beginning of the following row. Place the remaining 14 (16, 18) stitches on a holder.

BODY

With smaller needle, cast on 22 (24, 26) Front stitches, place marker to indicate right underarm, cast on 22 (24, 26) Back stitches, place marker to indicate left underarm and beginning of round—44 (48, 52) stitches. Join, being careful not to twist stitches.

RNDS 1–12: ★K1, p1; repeat from ★ around. Change to larger needle.
RND 13: P6 (7, 8), place marker, p3, k1, ssk, k1, p3, place marker, purl to end of round—43 (47, 51) stitches.
RND 14: Purl to first marker, work Row 1 of Bobble Vine Stitch Pattern across next 9 stitches, purl to end of round.

Continue in established pattern until Body measures 15¼" (38.5cm) from the beginning, ending last round 1 stitch before end of round.

DIVIDE BODY

Removing markers, bind off 2 stitches, work to 1 stitch before marker, bind off 2 stitches, purl to end of round—19 (21, 23) stitches remain for Front and 20 (22, 24) stitches remain for Back.

JOIN SLEEVES AND BODY

P14 (16, 18) Left Sleeve stitches, place marker to indicate raglan shaping, work 19 (21, 23) Front stitches, place marker to indicate raglan shaping, p14 (16, 18) Right Sleeve stitches, place marker to indicate raglan shaping, p20 (22, 24) Back stitches, place marker to indicate raglan shaping and beginning of round—67 (75, 83) stitches.

Work 2 rounds even.

NECK AND RAGLAN SHAPING

NOTE: READ ALL SHAPING INSTRUCTIONS BEFORE BEGINNING.

Continue in established pattern to short-row neck shaping, shaping as follows:

NEXT RND (DEC RND): ★P1, p2tog, work to 3 stitches before next shaping marker, ssp, p1, slip marker; repeat from ★ around—59 (67, 75) stitches.

Repeat Dec Rnd every 4 rounds twice, then every 3 rounds once, and every other round 1 (2, 3) time(s)—27 stitches remain when all raglan shaping is complete.

AT THE SAME TIME, when 4 (5, 6) Dec Rnds are complete, discontinue Bobble Vine Stitch Pattern and work short-row neck shaping as follows: ★work to 2 stitches from center front stitch, wrap and turn (see page 152); repeat from ★ once, ★★work to 6 stitches from center front, wrap and turn; repeat from ★★ once.

Continue on all stitches, picking up all wraps (see page 151), purl to left front marker.

COLLAR

NEXT ROW (DIVIDE FOR COLLAR): Removing markers, ★k5, inc1; repeat from ★ 4 times, k2, pick up and knit 5 stitches from inside edge of collar so that 5 stitches overlap at left front, turn—37 stitches. Change to smaller needle.
NEXT ROW (WS): P1, ★k1, p1; repeat from ★ to end.
NEXT ROW (BUTTONHOLE ROW): K1, p1, k1, yo, k2tog, work in pattern to end.

Work 18 more rows in established rib. Bind off.

FINISHING

Sew sleeve and underarm seams. Sew button to underlap of collar opposite buttonhole. Weave in ends.

Key

☐	K on RS, P on WS
⊟	P on RS, K on WS
●	MB
◫	T2R
◩	T2L

9-st panel

Twinkle Knit Bit

If the cord between knitting points on a pair of circular needles becomes tightly coiled or bent and difficult to use, run it under a steady stream of hot water from the faucet. As you do, hold the needles outstretched, grasping them by each end and directing the hot water all along the cord's length. Stop occasionally to massage the cord into proper shape.

BOOKBROWSER'S SWEATER SCHEMATIC

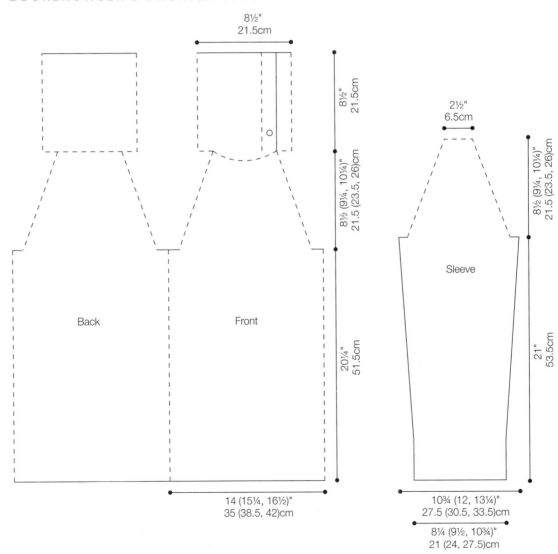

8½"
21.5cm

8½"
21.5cm

2½"
6.5cm

8½ (9¼, 10¼)"
21.5 (23.5, 26)cm

8½ (9¼, 10¼)"
21.5 (23.5, 26)cm

Back

Front

Sleeve

20¼"
51.5cm

21"
53.5cm

14 (15¼, 16½)"
35 (38.5, 42)cm

10¾ (12, 13¼)"
27.5 (30.5, 33.5)cm

8¼ (9½, 10¾)"
21 (24, 27.5)cm

Souvenir Shopping:
The Road Less Traveled

Have you ever discovered, while on holiday, a fabulous new food, household ware, beauty product, or a type of music you couldn't wait to share with those back home? Shopping for travel souvenirs doesn't always entail finding a perfect luxury good or one-of-a-kind antique. Instead, the charm of the quotidian might be just the ticket. Local versions of bespoke stationery, cleverly designed kitchen implements, wardrobe basics, costume jewelry, even hardware or hot sauces—especially those with cool packaging and graphics—make welcome presents and unique keepsakes.

Armed with a sense of adventure and a phrasebook, if needed, head to the local hardware store, notions shop, or market to comb through the offerings in search of eye-catching iterations of everyday useful items. (I have brought home plastic juicers, for example, from countries the world over, each one vastly different and bearing the mark of its home culture. Friends have received decorated purse mirrors from my journeys, as well.) Pretty hand towels, coin purses, and journals brought back from trips add a charming Twinkle touch to one's décor and make easily transported gifts that capture the joy of travel.

A side trip off the streets of fancy shops also puts you in touch with the local pulse and residents, where unexpected pleasures await. Once, in a hip Parisian antique shop, I asked the dealer for the name of the CD that he was playing and I was loving. Soon, I was escorted many blocks to a tiny music shop—absent from travel guides—that specialized in rare jazz recordings. The lesson? Twinkle travelers embrace a surprise discovery as much as a time-honored favorite restaurant, shop, or nightspot.

If in your amblings you don't come across such places, ask innkeepers, concierges, or friendly wait staff where they buy housewares. Sometimes you'll find treasures in local department stores. When in Paris, for example, try the lower-level housewares section of BHV Rivoli (on Rue de Rivoli, between Rue du Temple and Rue des Archives, in the 4th arrrondissement) for candy-colored drawer pulls, woven market bags, and weighty blocks of delicately scented hand soap in chic wrapping. Unless you're in the market for local-host gifts, though, think twice before scooping up the stylish, compact electric housewares that you only find in Europe; they require different voltage. Bear in mind, too, that materials of manufacture vary from place to place, so you'll want to find out if those painted café au lait bowls can withstand the dishwasher and microwave, whether you can use that hammered brass bowl for chips or just for non edibles such as flowers, or if the retro-looking pot of hand creme that caught your eye is just for show or good for pre-knitting moisturizing. (Likewise, remember that laws prohibit bringing home many unprocessed foods from abroad. You can, though, bring home things like wonderful canned charcuterie from Spain—mussels, white asparagus, or octopus, for example—or bagged fleur del sel from France, or fragrant vanilla beans from Mexico.)

Speaking of knitting, don't forget that the craft has devotees across the globe. Yarns and knitting tools aren't always sold in a yarn store as they often are in the US. Craft and notions shops in your holiday destinations often stock charming knitting paraphernalia such as needles, cases, or markers.

millbrook sweater dress

Page 28

The stylish Millbrook Sweater Dress is a cozy woolen cocoon that may render outerwear unnecessary. Its loose funnel neck, pulled in close on cool days, and set-in pockets might take the place of a scarf and mittens. The generous hip sizing permits ease of movement and contrasts with the snug bodice of this sweater. Note that the low armhole and wide neckline place the bust at the juncture of the underarm and body of the sweater—about two inches below the typical bustline—so don't be concerned by the scant bust dimensions of the finished knit garment. There's plenty of give to the yarn.

SIZES
XS (S, M, L)

Remember to use this guide to find your size based on your bust measurement: XS = 31"–33" (79cm–84cm); S = 34"–36" (86cm–91cm); M = 37"–39" (94cm–99cm); L = 40"–42" (102cm–107cm).

KNITTED MEASUREMENTS
Bust: 26½ (28½, 30, 31½)" (67 [72, 76, 82.5]cm)
Back length (not including collar): 31½ (32, 32, 32¼)" (79.5 [81, 81, 81.5]cm)

MATERIALS
6 (6, 7, 7) hanks Twinkle Handknits Soft Chunky, 100% virgin merino wool, 7 oz/200g, 83 yds/75m, #17 Dusty Rose 🔢6

US size 17 (12.75mm) 29" (75cm) circular needle

US size 19 (15mm) 29" (75cm) and 24" (60cm) circular needles or size needed to obtain gauge

Cable needle

Stitch holders

Stitch markers

Tapestry needle

GAUGE
11 stitches and 16½ rows = 7" (18cm) in Reverse Stockinette stitch on size 19 (15mm) needles.

Take time to check your gauge.

ABBREVIATIONS
Inc 1 (increase 1): Maintaining pattern, knit (or purl) 1 into right loop of stitch in row below next stitch on left-hand needle, then knit (or purl) the next stitch on left-hand needle.
T3R (twist 3 right): Slip next stitch onto cable needle and hold in back, k2, p1 from cable needle.
T3L (twist 3 left): Slip next 2 stitches onto cable needle and hold in front, p1, k2 from cable needle.
MB (make bobble): (K1, p1, k1) into next stitch, turn; p3, turn; k3tog.

NOTES
The sleeves are first worked back and forth on a circular needle; then, the body is worked in the round. The sleeves are joined to the body at the underarm and the sweater is knit in one piece from that point. Once charted pattern stitches are established, continue working chart in rows or rounds as appropriate, until neck shaping eliminates chart stitches. Mark the beginning of the round with a stitch marker.

RIGHT SLEEVE

With smaller needle, and using cable cast-on, cast on 5 (6, 6, 7) stitches, place marker, cast on 5 stitches, place marker, cast on 5 (6, 6, 7) stitches—15 (17, 17, 19) stitches.

ROW 1 (RS): P1, *k2, p2; repeat from * to end.
ROW 2: *K2, p2; repeat from * to last stitch, k1.
ROWS 3-4: Repeat Rows 1 and 2.

Change to larger needle and reverse stockinette stitch (see page 150).

NEXT ROW (INC ROW): P1, inc 1, purl to marker, slip marker, work Right Sleeve Pattern across next 5 stitches, slip marker, purl to last 2 stitches, inc 1, p1—17 (19, 19, 21) stitches.

Continuing in established patterns, work 6 rows even.

NEXT ROW (DEC ROW): P1, p2tog, work to last 3 stitches, ssp, p1—15 (17, 17, 19) stitches.

*Work 11 rows even, then repeat Inc Row—17 (19, 19, 21) stitches.

Repeat from * once more—19 (21, 21, 23) stitches.

Work even until Sleeve measures 19½" (24cm) from the beginning, ending with a right-side row.

UNDERARM SHAPING

Bind off 2 stitches at the beginning of the next row and 3 stitches at the beginning of the following row. Place the remaining 14 (16, 16, 18) stitches on holder.

LEFT SLEEVE

Work as for Right Sleeve, following chart for Left Sleeve Pattern across center 5 stitches.

BODY

With smaller needle, and using cable cast-on, cast on 44 (48, 52, 56) stitches, place marker to indicate left underarm and beginning of round. Join, being careful not to twist stitches.

NECK AND RAGLAN SHAPING TABLE		
	XS	S, M	L
RND 3		Fronts, Back, Sleeves	Fronts, Back, Sleeves
RND 4	Fronts, Back, Sleeves		
RND 5			
RND 6	Back	Fronts, Back, Sleeves	Fronts, Back, Sleeves
RND 7	Sleeves		
RND 8	Fronts. Cut yarn at end of rnd.		
RND/ROW 9	** see below Dec on Back only	Fronts, Back, Sleeves. Cut yarn at end of rnd.	Fronts, Back, Sleeves
RND/ROW 10	Bind off 1 stitch; Dec on Sleeves only	** see below	Work even. Cut yarn at end of rnd.
ROW 11	Bind off 1 stitch	Bind off 1 stitch; Dec on Fronts, Back and Sleeves	** see below Dec on Fronts, Back and Sleeves
ROW 12	Bind off 1 stitch; Dec on Fronts and Back only	Bind off 1 stitch	Bind off 1 stitch
ROW 13	Bind off 1 stitch; Dec on Sleeves only	Bind off 1 stitch; Dec on Back and Sleeves	Bind off 1 stitch; Dec on Fronts, Back and Sleeves
ROW 14	Skip to Collar	Bind off 1 stitch	Bind off 1 stitch
ROW 15	- -	Skip to Collar	Bind off 1 stitch; Dec on Back and Sleeves

** Slip first 5 (5, 5, 6) stitches to right-hand needle, place next 3 stitches on holder for center front neck. Sweater is worked back and forth in reverse stockinette stitch from this point. Rejoin yarn in next stitch and purl to end of row, decreasing at location indicated in table.

Work 24 rounds in k2, p2 rib.

Change to larger 29" (74cm) needle.

ROW 1 (RS): P1, M1-p, p1 (2, 3, 4), place marker to indicate edge of pocket, p2, M1-p, work Row 1 of Body Pattern over next 14 stitches, M1-p, p2; slip last 21 stitches worked to shorter needle for Pocket, turn—21 stitches.

Continuing to work back and forth on 21 Pocket stitches only, work 2 rows in established pattern.

NEXT ROW (DEC ROW): Ssk, work to last 2 stitches, k2tog—19 stitches.

[Work 3 rows even, then repeat Dec Row] twice—15 stitches.

Work 3 rows even. Cut yarn and let Pocket hang in front of work.

CONTINUE BODY
NOTE: READ THROUGH ALL SHAPING INSTRUCTIONS BEFORE BEGINNING.

With right side facing and returning to stitches on longer needle, long-tail cast-on 21 stitches onto right-hand needle, p2 (3, 4, 5), M1-p, place marker to indicate right underarm, ★p4 (5, 6, 6), M1-p; repeat from ★ 3 times, purl to end of round—53 (57, 61, 65) stitches.

Purl 11 (11, 10, 10) rounds.

NEXT RND (DEC RND): ★P1, p2tog; purl to 3 stitches before marker, ssp, p1, slip marker; repeat from ★ once more(49 (53, 57, 61) stitches.

Work 2 (2, 3, 3) rounds even.

JOIN POCKET
NEXT RND: P5 (6, 7, 8); holding needle with pocket stitches in front of and parallel to

left needle and maintaining pattern, [work together 1 stitch from front needle and 1 stitch from back needle] across next 15 stitches, purl to end of round.

Work 8 (8, 5, 5) rounds even (continuing cable pattern), then repeat Dec Rnd—45 (49, 53, 57) stitches.

Work 10 (10, 8, 8) rounds even, then repeat Dec Rnd—41 (45, 49, 53) stitches.

SIZES M AND L ONLY: Work 5 rounds even, then repeat Dec Rnd.

ALL SIZES: 21 (23, 23, 25) Front stitches and 20 (22, 22, 24) Back stitches remain when all shaping is complete.

Work even until Body measures approximately 26" (66cm), ending last round 2 stitches before beginning of round marker.

BODY UNDERARM SHAPING
RND 1: Removing markers, bind off next 4 stitches purlwise, work to 2 stitches before next marker, bind off 4 stitches purlwise, purl to end.

JOIN SLEEVES AND BODY
NOTE: READ THROUGH ALL SHAPING INSTRUCTIONS BEFORE BEGINNING

RND 2: P14 (16, 16, 18) Left Sleeve stitches, place marker to indicate raglan shaping, work 17 (19, 19, 21) Front stitches, place marker to indicate raglan shaping, p14 (16, 16, 18) Right Sleeve stitches, place marker to indicate raglan shaping, work 16 (18, 18, 20) Back stitches, place marker to indicate raglan shaping and beginning of round—61 (69, 69, 77) stitches.

NECK AND RAGLAN SHAPING
Work neck and raglan shaping on Fronts, Back, and Sleeves, placing decreases as indicated in Neck and Raglan Shaping Table on page 85 and working even on

rows where cells in the table are empty.

RS Rnds/Rows, if decrease precedes a marker: Ssp, p1, slip marker.

RS Rnds/Rows, if decrease follows a marker: Slip marker, p1, p2tog.

WS Rows, if decrease precedes a marker: K2tog, k1, slip marker.

WS Rows, if decrease follows a marker: Slip marker, k1, ssk.

All sizes: 24 stitches remain after all neck and raglan shaping is complete.

COLLAR
With right side facing and continuing to work in the round with shorter needle, pick up and knit 6 stitches along shaped neck edge to center front stitches, knit 3 stitches from holder, pick up and knit 7 stitches along shaped neck edge, place marker to indicate beginning of round—40 stitches.

Knit 31 rounds even. Bind off very loosely.

FINISHING
POCKET EDGES
With right side facing and using smaller needle, pick up and knit 12 stitches along one side of pocket opening.

ROW 1 (WS): P1, k2, (p2, k2) twice, end p1.

Work even in rib for 3 rows.

Bind off.

Repeat along other side of pocket opening.

Sew sleeve and underarm seams. Sew cast-on edge of pocket lining to wrong side of Front along top of ribbing. Sew down pocket edges. Weave in ends.

Key

K on RS, P on WS

P on RS, K on WS

K1-tbl on RS, P1-tbl on WS

MB

M1-P

T3R

T3L

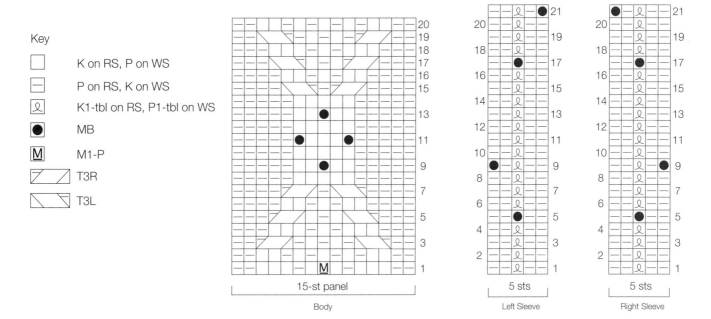

15-st panel

Body

5 sts

Left Sleeve

5 sts

Right Sleeve

MILLBROOK SWEATER DRESS SCHEMATIC

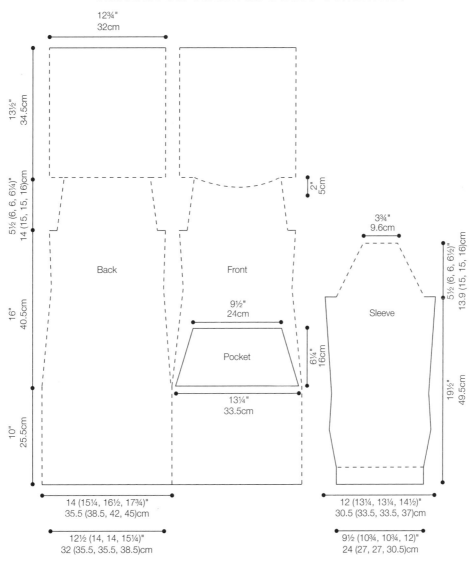

12¾"
32cm

13½"
34.5cm

5½ (6, 6, 6¼)"
14 (15, 15, 16)cm

16"
40.5cm

10"
25.5cm

Back

Front

2"
5cm

9½"
24cm

Pocket

6¼"
16cm

13¼"
33.5cm

14 (15¼, 16½, 17¾)"
35.5 (38.5, 42, 45)cm

12½ (14, 14, 15¼)"
32 (35.5, 35.5, 38.5)cm

3¾"
9.6cm

Sleeve

5½ (6, 6, 6½)"
13.9 (15, 15, 16)cm

19½"
49.5cm

12 (13¼, 13¼, 14½)"
30.5 (33.5, 33.5, 37)cm

9½ (10¾, 10¾, 12)"
24 (27, 27, 30.5)cm

vineyard potter's cardigan

page 28

This fitted cardigan's design details work together to produce a snug knit that hugs your form and brings to mind the fashion-forward look of a shrunken jacket. A wide ribbed hem and deep sleeve cuffs keep the material close to your body, and the regular trellis pattern and neat, ribbed collar both have structure to maintain the cardi's shape—this is not a knit that hangs loosely. The front panels climb over the shoulder to be seamed in the back, focusing attention on the bespoke trellis pattern.

SIZES
S (M, L)

Remember to use this guide to find your size based on your bust measurement: S = 34"–36" (86cm–91cm); M = 37"–39" (94cm–99cm); L = 40"–42" (102cm–107cm).

KNITTED MEASUREMENTS
Bust (buttoned): 33¾ (36¼, 38¾)" (85.5 [92, 97]cm)

Back length (not including collar): 22¼ (23, 23¾)" (56 [58, 60]cm)

MATERIALS
4 (5, 5) hanks Twinkle Handknits Soft Chunky, 100% virgin merino wool, 7 oz/200g, 83 yds/75m, #12 Riviera ⑥

US size 17 (12.75mm) 29" (75cm) circular needle

US size 19 (15mm) 29" (75cm) circular needle or size needed to obtain gauge

Stitch holders

Stitch markers

Tapestry needle

Five 1⅝" (4cm) buttons

GAUGE
11 stitches and 16½ rows = 7" (18cm) in reverse stockinette stitch on size 19 (15mm) needle.

Take the time to check your gauge.

ABBREVIATIONS
RT (right twist): Knit next 2 stitches together, leaving stitches on needle, knit first stitch, slip both stitches from needle.
LT (left twist): Slip next 2 stitches one at a time knitwise to the right-hand needle, then pass them back to the left-hand needle. Knit the 2nd stitch on the left-hand needle through back loop and leave stitch on needle, then knit 2 together through back loop; slip both stitches from needle.
RS Dec Row: P2tog, purl to last 2 stitches, ssp.
WS Dec Row: Ssk, knit to last 2 stitches, k2tog.
Inc Row (RS or WS row): Work 1 stitch (k or p), inc 1, work to last 2 stitches, inc 1, work 1 stitch.

Trellis Stitch Pattern (10-stitch panel; see chart, page 90)
ROW 1 (RS): K1, yo, ssk, k2tog, (yo) twice, ssk, k2tog, yo, k1.
ROW 2: P1, k1, p2; knit into front and back of double yarn-over, p2, k1, p1.
ROW 3: K1, p1, RT, p2, RT, p1, k1.
ROW 4: P1, k1, p2, k2, p2, k1, p1.

ROW 5: K1, *k2tog, (yo) twice, ssk; repeat from * once, end k1.
ROW 6: P2, *knit into front and back of double yarn-over, p2; repeat from * once.
ROW 7: K2, p2, RT, p2, k2.
ROW 8: P2, *k2, p2; repeat from * once.
Repeat Rows 1–8 for pattern.

Right Trellis Pattern Stitch (10-stitch panel; see chart, page 90)
ROW 1 (RS): K1, yo, ssk, k2tog, (yo) twice, ssk, k2tog, yo, k1.
ROW 2: P1, k1, p2; knit into front and back of double yarn-over, p2, k1, p1.
ROW 3: K1, p1, LT, p2, LT, p1, k1.
ROW 4: P1, k1, p2, k2, p2, k1, p1.
ROW 5: K1, *k2tog, (yo) twice, ssk; repeat from * once, end k1.
ROW 6: P2, *knit into front and back of double yarnover, p2; repeat from * once.
ROW 7: K2, p2, LT, p2, k2.
ROW 8: P2, *k2, p2; repeat from * once.
Repeat Rows 1–8 for pattern.

NOTES
The sleeves and body are worked back and forth; a circular needle is used to accommodate the many stitches. When working neck shaping, maintain established Trellis Stitch Pattern. The Fronts are worked without shoulder shaping, throwing the shoulder seam to the back.

BODY
With smaller needle, and using cable cast-on, cast on 12 (13, 14) stitches, place marker to indicate right underarm, cable cast on 25 (27, 29) stitches, place marker to indicate left underarm, cable cast on 12 (13, 14) stitches—49 (53, 57) stitches.

ROW 1 (RS): P1, *k1, p1; repeat from *.

Continue in established rib for 17 more rows. Change to larger needle.

NEXT ROW (RS): P0 (1, 1), work Left Trellis Stitch across next 10 stitches, *purl to marker, slip marker; repeat from * once, p0 (1, 2), work Right Trellis Stitch across next 10 stitches, end p0 (1, 1).

Work even in established pattern, keeping edge stitches in reverse stockinette stitch (see page 00), until Body measures 14½" (37cm) from beginning, ending with a WS row.

DIVIDE BODY
Next row (RS): Removing markers, work to 2 stitches before marker, ssp, place these 11 (12, 13) Right Front stitches on holder, p2tog, work to 2 stitches before marker, ssp, place these 23 (25, 27) Back stitches on holder, p2tog, work to end—11 (12, 13) Left Front stitches.

LEFT FRONT
Work 1 row even.

NEXT ROW (RS): P2tog, work to end of row—10 (11, 12) stitches.

Work 8 (10, 12) rows even, ending with a right-side row.

Bind off 2 stitches at the beginning of the next row and 2 stitches at the beginning of the following wrong-side row—6 (7, 8) stitches.

Work 4 rows even. Bind off.

BACK
Place 23 (25, 27) Back stitches onto needle.

With wrong side facing, knit 1 row.

Work RS Dec Row—21 (23, 25) stitches.

Work 10 (12, 13) rows even.

BACK SHOULDER SHAPING
Working RS Dec Rows or WS Dec Rows as appropriate, decrease 1 stitch at each side on the next 5 (5, 6) rows. Bind off the remaining 11 (13, 13) stitches.

RIGHT FRONT
Place 11 (12, 13) Right Front stitches onto needle.

With wrong side facing, work 1 row.

NEXT ROW (RS): Work to last 2 stitches, k2tog—10 (11, 12) stitches.

Work 9 (11, 13) rows even, ending with a wrong-side row.

Bind off 2 stitches at the beginning of the next row and 2 stitches at the beginning of the following right-side row—6 (7, 8) stitches.

Work 3 rows even. Bind off.

SLEEVES (MAKE 2)
With smaller needle, using cable cast-on method (see page 00), cast on 15 (17, 17) stitches.

ROW 1 (RS): K1, *p1, k1; repeat from * across.

Continue in established rib for 19 more rows, ending with a wrong-side row.

Change to larger needle and reverse stockinette stitch.

Working RS Inc Rows or WS Inc Rows as appropriate, increase 1 stitch at each side on the next row, then every 4 rows 0 (0, 1) times, and every 7 rows once—19 (21, 23) stitches.

Work even until Sleeve measures 15¼" (38.5cm) from the beginning, ending with a wrong-side row.

SLEEVE CAP

Working RS Dec Rows or WS Dec Rows as appropriate, decrease 1 stitch at each side on the next row, then every 3 rows twice, and every other row 2 (2, 3) times—9 (11, 11) stitches.

FINISHING

Sew front shoulders to shaped back shoulders.

NECK BAND

With right side facing and using smaller needle, pick up and knit 29 (31, 33) stitches along the neck edge.

Work in k1, p1 rib (see page 150) for 5 rows.

Bind off knitwise on right side.

BUTTON BAND

With right side facing and using smaller needle, pick up and knit 37 stitches down Left Front edge, including side of Neck Band.

Work in k1, p1 rib for 5 rows.

Bind off knitwise on right side.

BUTTONHOLE BAND

With right side facing and using smaller needle, pick up and knit 37 stitches up Right Front edge, including side of Neck Band.

NEXT ROW (WS): K1, *p1, k1; repeat from * to end.

Buttonhole Row (RS): P1, k1, *yo, k2tog, (p1, k1) 3 times; repeat from * to last 3 stitches, yo, k2tog, p1.

Work 2 more rows in rib as established.

Bind off knitwise on right side.

Sew in sleeves, easing in extra fullness to create a puffed sleeve cap. Sew sleeve seams. Weave in ends. Sew on buttons, creating shanks if necessary to accommodate the thickness of the knit fabric.

Key

☐	K on RS, P on WS
⊟	P on RS, K on WS
⊡	K1-tbl on WS
◿	RT
○	YO
◺	LT
◹	SSK
◹	K2tog

LEFT FRONT

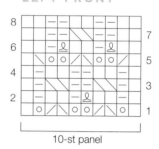

10-st panel

RIGHT FRONT

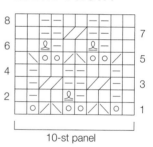

10-st panel

VINEYARD POTTER'S CARDIGAN SCHEMATIC

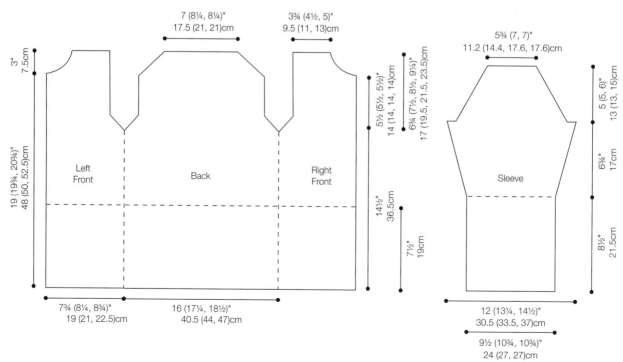

7 (8¼, 8¼)"
17.5 (21, 21)cm

3¾ (4½, 5)"
9.5 (11, 13)cm

5½ (5½, 5½)"
14 (14, 14)cm

6¾ (7½, 8½, 9¼)"
17 (19.5, 21.5, 23.5)cm

3"
7.5cm

19 (19¾, 20¾)"
48 (50, 52.5)cm

14½"
36.5cm

Left Front

Back

Right Front

7½"
19cm

7¾ (8¼, 8¾)"
19 (21, 22.5)cm

16 (17¼, 18½)"
40.5 (44, 47)cm

5¾ (7, 7)"
11.2 (14.4, 17.6, 17.6)cm

5 (5, 6)"
13 (13, 15)cm

6¾"
17cm

Sleeve

8½"
21.5cm

12 (13¼, 14½)"
30.5 (33.5, 37)cm

9½ (10¾, 10¾)"
24 (27, 27)cm

bennington jumper dress

page 30

Remarkably modern and hip, this dress is worked on circular needles, first in the round at the hem, then back and forth through the intarsia panel, after which the fabric is rejoined and continued in the round to the underarm. The yoke, split in front and lace-tied, is rendered in charming garter stripes that contrast with the body's stockinette fabric, giving this knit its handcrafted, vintage vibe. Read the yoke instructions carefully, plotting out the rows on which you will be working the eyelets for the laces, raglan shoulder decreases, and short rows that contour the neckline. Throughout the chest area, negative ease creates a flatteringly firm bodice. Given this pattern's low armhole, the bust is situated where the underarm joins the body, about two inches below the usual bustline. Therefore, small bust dimensions for the finished garment are to be expected. Hiding behind those placid, pretty curves in the yoke is some subtle knitted tailoring!

SIZES

XS (S, M, L)

Remember to use this guide to find your size based on your bust measurement: XS = 31"–33" (79cm–84cm); S = 34"–36" (86cm–91cm); M = 37"–39" (94cm–99cm); L = 40"–42" (102cm–107cm).

KNITTED MEASUREMENTS

Bust: 24¼ (26¾, 29¼, 31¾)" (61 [67.5, 74, 80.5]cm)

Back length: 40½" (102.5cm)

MATERIALS

3 (3, 3, 3) hanks Twinkle Handknits Soft Chunky, 100% virgin merino wool, 7 oz/200g, 83 yds/75m, #25 Powder (A); 1 skein each in #03 Crimson (B), #14 Sapphire (C) and #12 Riviera (D) (6)

US size 17 (12.75mm) 29" (75cm) circular needle

US size 19 (15mm) 24" (60cm) and 29" (75cm) circular needles or size needed to obtain gauge

Size K-10½ (6.5mm) crochet hook

Stitch holders

Stitch markers

Tapestry needle

GAUGE

11 stitches and 16½ rows = 7" (18cm) in stockinette stitch on size 19 (15mm) needles.

Take the time to check your gauge.

The body is knit back and forth throughout the intarsia section, then joined and worked in the round to the underarms. The sleeve/yoke section is worked back and forth. A circular needle is used to accommodate the many stitches; work back and forth in rows or in the round as indicated. The front neck drop is formed by short rows. These short rows are counted like full rows when you are determining where to make decreases for raglan shaping. Mark the beginning of the round with a stitch marker in a color different from the others.

BODY

With smaller needle and C, cast on 71 stitches.

Place marker for beginning of round and join, being careful not to twist stitches.

Work 6 rounds in k1, p1 rib.

Change to larger needle and stockinette stitch (see page 150).

Work Intarsia Chart through Row 24. (see page 95)

JOIN BODY

RND 1: With A, k10, place marker to indicate front shaping, k15, place marker to indicate front shaping, k10, place marker to indicate right underarm, k10, place marker to indicate back shaping, k15, place marker to indicate back shaping, k9, k2tog, place marker to indicate beginning of round—70 stitches.

RNDS 2-7: Knit.

BODY SHAPING

NOTE: READ ALL SHAPING INSTRUCTIONS BEFORE BEGINNING.

RS RNDS/ROWS, IF DECREASE PRECEDES A MARKER: K2tog, k1, slip marker.

RS RNDS/ROW, IF DECREASE FOLLOWS A MARKER: Slip marker, k1, ssk.

WS ROWS, IF DECREASE PRECEDES A MARKER: Ssp, p1, slip marker.

WS ROWS, IF DECREASE FOLLOWS A MARKER: Slip marker, p1, p2tog.

Continue working in the round, making decreases at underarms and on either side of front and back shaping markers as indicated in table below and working even on rounds where cells are empty.

BODY SHAPING TABLE				
	XS	S	M	L
RND 8	Front and Back underarms	Front and Back underarms		
RND 9				
RND 10			Front and Back underarms	
RND 11				Front and Back underarms
RND 12	Front and Back shaping markers	Front and Back shaping markers	Front and Back shaping markers	Front and Back shaping markers
RND 13				
RND 14	Front and Back underarms			
RND 15				
RND 16		Front and Back underarms		
RND 17				
RND 18				
RND 19				
RND 20	Front and Back underarms			
RND 21	Front and Back shaping markers	Front and Back shaping markers	Front and Back shaping markers	Front and Back shaping markers

ALL SIZES

42 (46, 50, 50) stitches remain when all decreases are complete.

Work 1 round even, removing front and back shaping markers on last round.

NEXT RND (ESTABLISH RIBBED PANELS):

SIZE S ONLY

(K1, p1) twice, k15, (p1, k1) twice, slip marker, (k1, p1) to end of round.

ALL OTHER SIZES

(K1, p1) 2 (–, 3, 3) times, k13, (p1, k1) 2 (–, 3, 3) times, slip marker, (k1, p1) to end of round.

Work 7 rounds even in established pattern.

		XS	S	M	L
	EYELET ROWS AND RAGLAN SHAPING TABLE				
ROW 3	Eyelet Row	Front, Back, and Sleeves	Front, Back, and Sleeves	Front, Back, and Sleeves	Front, Back, and Sleeves
ROW 4					
ROW 5				Sleeves	Front, Back, and Sleeves
ROW 6					
ROW 7		Back and Sleeves	Front, Back, and Sleeves	Front and Back	
ROW 8				Sleeves	Front, Back, and Sleeves
ROW 9	Eyelet Row				
ROW 10					
ROW 11		Front, Back, and Sleeves	Front, Back, and Sleeves	Front, Back, and Sleeves	Front, Back, and Sleeves
ROW 12					
ROW 13					
ROW 14					
ROW 15	Eyelet Row	Sleeves	Back and Sleeves	Front, Back, and Sleeves	Front, Back, and Sleeves
ROW 16					
ROW 17					
ROW 18**					
ROW 19		Front, Back, and Sleeves	Front and Sleeves	Sleeves	Sleeves
ROW 20					
ROW 21					
ROW 22					
ROW 23		Back and Sleeves	Back and Sleeves	Front, Back, and Sleeves	Front, Back, and Sleeves

SIZES XS, S, AND M ONLY
K4, k2tog, k9 (11, 13, -), k2tog, k4, slip marker, k4, k2tog, k9 (11, 13, -), k2 tog, k4.

SIZE L
Knit 1 round.
ALL SIZES: 38 (42, 46, 50) stitches remain.

Work 8 rounds even in stockinette stitch, ending 2 stitches before beginning of round marker.

DIVIDE BODY
NEXT RND: Removing markers, bind off 4 stitches, knit to 2 stitches before next marker, bind off 4 stitches, knit to end of round—15 (17, 19, 21) stitches each for Front and Back. Cut A.

CREATE SLEEVE CAPS
Slip next 7 (8, 9, 10) Front stitches to right needle.

ROW 1 (RS): With A, bind off 1 stitch, knit remaining Front stitches, place marker for raglan shaping; turn work and, beginning with last stitch knit, using cable cast-on method (see page 00), cast on purlwise 16 (16, 18, 20) Right Sleeve stitches, turn work; place marker for raglan shaping, k15 (17, 19, 21) Back stitches, place marker for raglan shaping, turn work; beginning with last stitch knit, cable cast on purlwise 16 (16, 18, 20) Left Sleeve stitches, place marker for raglan shaping, knit remaining Front stitches—61 (65, 73, 81) stitches. Turn.

ROW 2: Knit. Change to B.

Continue in alternating Garter stitch stripes (2 rows A, 2 rows B as established) until a total of 8 stripes are complete, then change to A and work in stockinette stitch to end.

AT THE SAME TIME, work eyelet rows and raglan shaping on Fronts, Back, and Sleeves (working decreases before and after markers as for Body Shaping above) as indicated in the Eyelet Rows and Raglan Shaping Table on page 93, and working even on rows where cells are empty.

EYELET ROW (RS): K1, k2tog, yo, work in established pattern to last 3 stitches, yo, ssk, k1.

ALSO AT THE SAME TIME on Row marked ★★, begin short rows as follows, maintaining raglan shaping:

Work to 3 stitches from Left Front edge, wrap and turn; work to 3 stitches from Right Front edge, wrap and turn; work to 6 stitches from Left Front edge, wrap and turn; work to 6 stitches from Right Front edge, wrap and turn. Continue on all stitches, picking up all wraps.

ALL SIZES
23 (23, 25, 29) stitches remain when all shaping is complete.

Work 4 rows even in stockinette stitch. Bind off loosely.

FINISHING
Sew side seam on intarsia section, using ½ stitch at each side edge for the seam. Weave in ends.

With crochet hook and A, crochet a chain 40" (101.5cm) long. Fasten off. Using the photo as a guide (see page 91), thread the chain through the eyelets.

BENNINGTON JUMPER DRESS SCHEMATIC

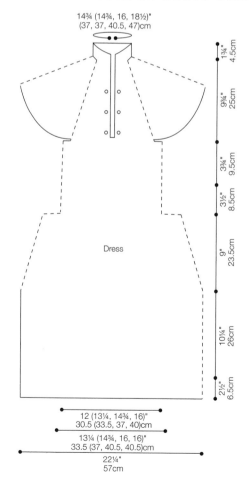

14¾ (14¾, 16, 18½)"
(37, 37, 40.5, 47)cm

1¾"
4.5cm

9¾"
25cm

3¾"
9.5cm

3½"
8.5cm

9"
23.5cm

Dress

10¼"
26cm

2½"
6.5cm

12 (13¼, 14¾, 16)"
30.5 (33.5, 37, 40)cm

13¼ (14¾, 16, 16)"
33.5 (37, 40.5, 40.5)cm

22¼"
57cm

Color Key

☐ #25 Powder

■ #03 Crimson

■ #14 Sapphire

■ #50 Teal

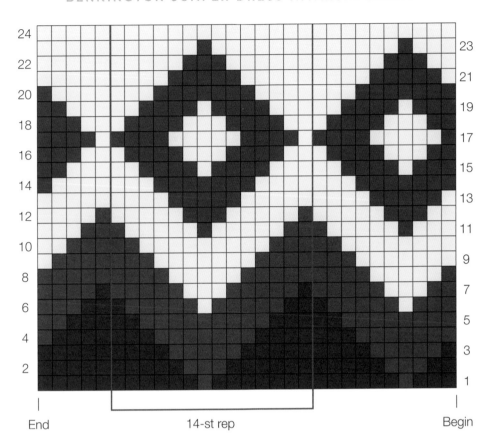

End   14-st rep   Begin

Twinkle Knit Bit

When knitting on holiday, plan ahead a little. If you're flying, visit the Transportation Security Administration's Web site for updates on restricted items (http://www.tsa.gov/travelers/airtravel/assistant/editorial_1252.shtm). Currently, many knitting items are permissible on airplanes, including short knitting needles (circular needles with cables measuring less than 20 inches in length) and blunt-tipped sewing scissors. Nonetheless, some items may be deemed unfit for carry-on or even checked baggage at the discretion of the supervising TSA employee. Carrying a self-addressed, stamped envelope to ship home any items unexpectedly prohibited at the airport is one way to safeguard beloved knitting tools. Likewise, threading a strand of yarn through your live stitches in case you have to surrender needles at security is also a good idea (you can pack extra needles in your checked bag to use at your destination). Anecdotal evidence suggests shorter, dull-tipped needles—especially nonmetal ones—may be the wisest choices. Circular needles are handy for travel: They let you keep your work close to your body and out of the way. To streamline your in-flight project bag, store yarns in self-sealing bags with clipped corners so you can thread out the working end, keeping the rest of the ball tidy and anchored in your carry-on. You can reinforce the hole, if necessary, with reinforcing stickers made for hole-punched paper, or simply use pull-zipper plastic bags that can be kept open enough to thread out the yarn end. Include a self-sealing bag big enough to hold your in-progress project (so it stays clean during security inspection and while traveling), a photocopy of your project pattern, and a small bag holding essential tools.

vintner's sweater

page 30

Work the body of this form-fitting, sexy knit in the round on circular needles from the striped hem to the waist. There, you'll switch to a 1 x 1 rib that widens in the center to shape the bodice—thanks to short rows—almost like a bustier. More short rows follow to fill out the bust and carve the deep neckline, and then the sleeves are picked up and the garment is knit as a whole, in the round. Making raglan decreases and short rows together sculpts the Vintner's Sweater further for the snug, shapely fit required to hold the upper body in place. Rest assured that the finished knit, surprisingly small when laid flat, will expand for proper fit.

SIZES

XS (S, M, L)

Remember to use this guide to find your size based on your bust measurement: XS = 31"–33" (79cm–84cm); S = 34"–36" (86cm–91cm); M = 37"–39" (94cm–99cm); L = 40"–42" (102cm–107cm).

KNITTED MEASUREMENTS

Bust: 20$\frac{1}{2}$ (23, 25$\frac{1}{2}$, 28)" (52 [58.5, 64.5, 70.5]cm)

Back length: 23$\frac{1}{2}$ (24, 24$\frac{1}{4}$, 24$\frac{3}{4}$)" (59.5 [61, 61.5, 62.5]cm)

MATERIALS

2 (3, 3, 3) hanks Twinkle Handknits Soft Chunky, 100% virgin merino wool, 7 oz/200g, 83 yds/75m, #12 Riviera (A); 1 skein each in #14 Sapphire (B) and #25 Powder (C) 6

US size 19 (15mm) 29" (75cm) and 24" (60cm) circular needles or size needed to obtain gauge

Stitch holders

Stitch markers

Tapestry needle

GAUGE

11 stitches and 16$\frac{1}{2}$ rows = 7" (18cm) in reverse stockinette stitch on size 19 (15mm) needles.

Take the time to check your gauge.

NOTES

First, the sleeves are worked back and forth on a circular needle; then the body is worked in the round. The sleeves are joined to the body at the underarm, and the sweater is knit in one piece from that point. The deep front neckline is formed by short rows beginning before the sleeve join; count these short rows like full ones when you are determining where to make decreases for the raglan shaping. Mark the beginning of the round with a stitch marker in a color different from the others.

SLEEVES (MAKE 2)

With either needle and A, cable cast on 21 (21, 21, 23) stitches.

ROW 1 (RS): P1, *k1, p1; repeat from * to end.
ROW 2: K1, *p1, k1; repeat from * to end.
ROW 3: With B, purl, increasing 8 (10, 10, 8) stitches evenly spaced across row—29 (31, 31, 31) stitches.
ROW 4: With B, knit.

Continuing in reverse stockinette stitch, work 2 rows in A, then 2 rows in B. Cut B.

With A, work 6 rows even.

UNDERARM SHAPING

Bind off 2 stitches at the beginning of the next 2 rows. Place the remaining 25 (27, 27, 27) stitches on holder.

BODY

With longer needle and B, cast on 56 (60, 64, 68) stitches; place marker to indicate center front and beginning of round. Join, being careful not to twist stitches.

RNDS 1–5: Knit.
RND 6: With A, purl.
RND 7: With C, knit.
RND 8: With A, purl.
RND 9: With C, knit.
RND 10: With A, purl.
RND 11: With C, purl.
RNDS 12–20: With A, purl.
RND 21: Purl, decreasing 24 stitches (p2tog) evenly spaced around—32 (36, 40, 44) stitches.
RND 22: Working in k1, p1 rib (see page 150), work 8 (9, 10, 11) stitches, place marker to indicate right underarm, work 16 (18, 20, 22) stitches, place marker to indicate left underarm, work to end of round.

Work 9 more rounds in k1, p1 rib, then shape front rib by working short rows as follows:

Maintaining rib pattern, *work to 4 stitches beyond center front marker, wrap and turn; repeat from * once; **work to 8 stitches beyond center front marker, wrap and turn (see Short Rows on page 152); repeat from ** once. Continue on all stitches, picking up all wraps (see page 151).

Purl 4 rounds, turn work.

NOTE: READ ALL SHAPING INSTRUCTIONS FIRST.

BEGIN FRONT NECK SHAPING

ROW 1 (WS): Knit to 2 stitches before center front marker, wrap and turn.

ROW 2 (RS): Purl to 2 stitches before center front marker, wrap and turn.

ROW 3: Knit to 3 stitches before center front marker, wrap and turn.

ROW 4: Purl to 3 stitches before center front marker, wrap and turn.

Working back and forth with short-row shaping as established, wrap and turn 1 stitch farther away from center front marker on next 6 (4, 4, 4) rows, 2 stitches farther away from center front marker on next 8 (10, 12, 14) rows. When short-row-shaping is complete, continue working on all stitches, picking up all wraps.

AT THE SAME TIME, when 8 rounds beyond ribbing have been completed, divide body as follows:

DIVIDE BODY

ROW 1 (RS): *Purl to 2 stitches before underarm marker, bind off next 4 stitches purlwise (removing marker); repeat from * once, purl to end of round as appropriate for short-row shaping.

JOIN SLEEVES AND BODY

ROW 2: Continuing short-row neck shaping, knit to bound off-stitches, place marker to indicate raglan shaping, k25 (27, 27, 27) Left Sleeve stitches, place marker to indicate raglan shaping, k12 (14, 16, 18) Back stitches, place marker to indicate raglan shaping, k25 (27, 27, 27) Right Sleeve stitches, place marker to indicate raglan shaping, knit to end of round as appropriate for short-row shaping—74 (82, 86, 90) stitches

RAGLAN SHAPING

Following Raglan Shaping Table on page 98 through Row 16 (16, 16, 17), work raglan shaping and continue short-row neck shaping at the same time, making mirrored decreases according to the location of the decrease. Work even where cells in the table are empty.

RS Rows, if decrease precedes a marker: Ssp, p1, slip marker.
RS Rows, if decrease follows a marker: Slip marker, p1, p2tog.
WS Rows, if decrease precedes a marker: K2tog, k1, slip marker.
WS Rows, if decrease follows a marker: Slip marker, k1, ssk.
When all shaping is complete, 36 (40, 40, 42) stitches remain. Bind off very loosely all around, picking up all wraps.

FINISHING

Sew sleeve and underarm seams. Weave in ends.

	XS	S	M	L
ROW 3	Sleeves	Front and Sleeves	Front and Sleeves	Front and Sleeves
ROW 4	Back and Sleeves	Back and Sleeves	Back and Sleeves	Back and Sleeves
ROW 5	Sleeves	Sleeves	Sleeves	Front and Sleeves
ROW 6	Sleeves	Sleeves	Sleeves	Sleeves
ROW 7	Sleeves (Back edge only)	Sleeves (Back edge only)	Sleeves (Back edge only)	Sleeves (Back edge only)
ROW 8	Back and Sleeves (Back edge only)	Back and Sleeves (Back edge only)	Back and Sleeves (Back edge only)	Back and Sleeves (Back edge only)
ROW 9	Sleeves (Back edge only)	Sleeves (Back edge only)	Sleeves (Back edge only)	Sleeves (Back edge only)
ROW 10	Sleeves (Back edge only)	Sleeves (Back edge only)	Sleeves (Back edge only)	Sleeves (Back edge only)
ROW 11	Sleeves (Back edge only)	Sleeves (Back edge only)	Sleeves (Back edge only)	Sleeves (Back edge only)
ROW 12	Back and Sleeves (Back edge only)	Back and Sleeves (Back edge only)	Back and Sleeves (Back edge only)	Back and Sleeves (Back edge only)
ROW 13	Sleeves (Back edge only)	Sleeves (Back edge only)	Sleeves (Back edge only)	Sleeves (Back edge only)
ROW 14	Sleeves (Back edge only)	Sleeves (Back edge only)	Back and Sleeves (Back edge only)	Back and Sleeves (Back edge only)
ROW 15		Sleeves (Back edge only)	Sleeves (Back edge only)	Sleeves (Back edge only)
ROW 16			Sleeves (Back edge only)	Sleeves (Back edge only)
ROW 17	Go to Bind-off			
ROW 18		Go to Bind-off		
ROW 19			Go to Bind-off	

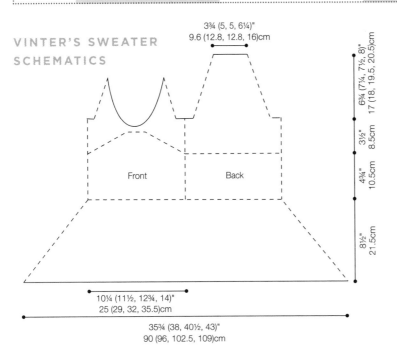

VINTER'S SWEATER
SCHEMATICS

3¾ (5, 5, 6¼)"
9.6 (12.8, 12.8, 16)cm

6¾ (7¼, 7½, 8)"
17 (18, 19.5, 20.5)cm

3½"
8.5cm

4¾"
10.5cm

Front   Back

8½"
21.5cm

10¼ (11½, 12¾, 14)"
25 (29, 32, 35.5)cm

35¾ (38, 40½, 43)"
90 (96, 102.5, 109)cm

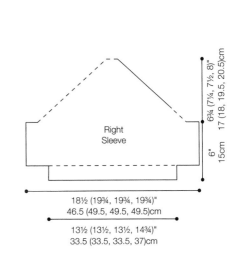

Right Sleeve

6¾ (7¼, 7½, 8)"
17 (18, 19.5, 20.5)cm

6"
15cm

18½ (19¾, 19¾, 19¾)"
46.5 (49.5, 49.5, 49.5)cm

13½ (13½, 13½, 14¾)"
33.5 (33.5, 33.5, 37)cm

holyoke sweater

page 32

Big stitches blow up the overlapping stripes to great graphic effect—they almost look pixelated—in this Twinkle reworking of a popular favorite. The Holyoke is made using a treasured Twinkle design method—knitting sleeves back and forth and joining them at the underarms to a body worked in the round, then knitting the remainder as a whole. Raglan shaping at the shoulders relies upon traditional decreases (the right-slanting "k2tog" and the left-slanting "ssk") but, when combined with short-row shaping, the softly curved knitted fabric lets the stripes span the yoke with uncommon grace. Colorful yet refined, it makes a great travel sweater and an impressive swift-to-gift pattern.

SIZES
S (M, L)

Remember to use this guide to find your size based on your bust measurement: S = 34"–36" (86cm–91cm); M = 37"–39" (94cm–99cm); L = 40"–42" (102cm–107cm).

KNITTED MEASUREMENTS
Bust: 30½ (33, 35½)" (77 [83.5, 90]cm)

Back length (not including collar): 21 (21¼, 21¾)" (53 [54, 55]cm)

MATERIALS
3 (3, 3) hanks Twinkle Handknits Soft Chunky, 100% virgin merino wool, 7 oz/200g, 83 yds/75m, #03 Crimson (A); 1 skein each in #08 White (B), #07 Canary (C), #09 Black (D), and #20 Icy Blue (E) [6]

US size 19 (15mm) 29" (75cm) and 24" (60cm) circular needles or size needed to obtain gauge

Stitch holders

Stitch markers

Tapestry needle

GAUGE
11 stitches and 16½ rows = 7" (18cm) in stockinette stitch on size 19 (15mm) needles.

Take the time to check your gauge.

ABBREVIATION
Inc 1 (increase 1): Maintaining pattern, knit (or purl) 1 into right loop of stitch in row below next stitch on left-hand needle, then knit (or purl) the next stitch on left-hand needle.

NOTES
First, the sleeves are worked back and forth on a circular needle, then the body is worked in the round. The sleeves are joined to the body at the underarm and the sweater is knit in one piece from that point; change to a shorter circular needle when it is comfortable to do so. The front neck drop is formed by working short rows. These short rows are counted like full rows when you are determining where to make decreases for raglan shaping. One stitch marker should be a color different from the others to indicate the beginning of round.

SLEEVES (MAKE 2)

With shorter needle and A, using cable cast-on, cast on 13 (15, 17) stitches.

ROW 1 (RS): K1, *p1, k1; repeat from * across.

Continue in established rib for 3 more rows.

Change to stockinette stitch and work 8 rows even.

NEXT ROW (INC ROW): K1, inc 1, knit to last stitch, inc 1, k1—15 (17, 19) stitches.

Work 11 rows even, then repeat Inc Row—17 (19, 21) stitches.

Work 10 rows even, then repeat Inc Row—19 (21, 23) stitches.

Work 1 row even.

UNDERARM SHAPING

Bind off 2 stitches at the beginning of the next row and 1 stitch at the beginning of the following row. Place the remaining 16 (18, 20) stitches on holder.

BODY

With longer needle and A, cast on 24 (26, 28) Back stitches, place marker to indicate left underarm, cast on 24 (26, 28) Front stitches, place marker to indicate right underarm and beginning of round—48 (52, 56) stitches. Join, being careful not to twist stitches. Work 8 rounds in k1, p1, rib. Change to stockinette stitch and work even until Body measures 12 3/4" (32.5cm)

NECK AND RAGLAN SHAPING TABLE

	S	M	L
RND 1		Front, Back, and Sleeves	Front, Back, and Sleeves
RND 2	Front, Back, and Sleeves		
RND 3			
RND 4		Front, Back, and Sleeves	Front, Back, and Sleeves
RND 5			
RND 6	Front, Back, and Sleeves		
RND 7		Front, Back, and Sleeves	Front, Back, and Sleeves
RND 8**			
RND 9			
RND 10	Front, Back, and Sleeves	Front, Back, and Sleeves	Front, Back, and Sleeves
RND 11			
RND 12			Front and Back
RND 13	Front, Back, and Sleeves	Front, Back, and Sleeves	Sleeves
RND 14			Front and Back
RND 15		Front, Back, and Sleeves	Sleeves
RND 16	Front, Back, and Sleeves		Front and Back
RND 17	Front	Front	Sleeves
RND 18	Back and Sleeves		Front
RND 19	Beg Collar	Back and Sleeves	
RND 20		Beg Collar	Back and Sleeves

from the beginning, ending 1 stitch before beginning of round marker.

DIVIDE BODY

Removing underarm markers, bind off 2 stitches, knit to 1 stitch before underarm marker, bind off 2 stitches, knit to end of round—22 (24, 26) stitches each for Front and Back.

JOIN SLEEVES AND BODY

Knit 16 (18, 20) Right Sleeve stitches, place marker to indicate raglan shaping, knit 22 (24, 26) Back stitches, place marker to indicate raglan shaping, knit 16 (18, 20) Left Sleeve stitches, place marker to indicate raglan shaping, knit 11 (12, 13) left Front stitches, place marker to indicate center front, knit 11 (12, 13) right Front stitches, place marker to indicate raglan shaping and beginning of round—76 (84, 92) stitches.

NECK AND RAGLAN SHAPING

NOTE: READ ALL SHAPING INSTRUCTIONS BEFORE BEGINNING.

RS RNDS/ROWS, IF RAGLAN DECREASE PRECEDES A MARKER: Work to 3 stitches before marker, k2tog, k1, slip marker.

RS RNDS/ROWS, IF RAGLAN DECREASE FOLLOWS A MARKER: Slip marker, k1, ssk.

Begin color chart below; when chart is complete, continue with color E to end.

AT THE SAME TIME, work raglan shaping on Fronts, Back and Sleeves, placing decreases as indicated in the Neck and Raglan Shaping Table (see page 100) and working even on rounds where cells are empty.

ALSO AT THE SAME TIME, on rounds marked ★★, work short rows as follows, maintaining raglan shaping:

Work to 3 stitches from center front, wrap and turn (see Short Rows on page 52); repeat from ★ once. ★Work to 5 stitches from center front, wrap and turn; repeat from ★ once. Continue on all stitches, picking up all wraps (see page 151).

ALL SIZES

28 (28, 28, 28) stitches remain when all shaping is complete.

COLLAR

Work 12 rounds even. Bind off very loosely.

FINISHING

Sew sleeve and underarm seams. Weave in ends.

HOLYOKE SWEATER COLOR CHART

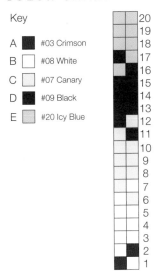

Key

A #03 Crimson
B #08 White
C #07 Canary
D #09 Black
E #20 Icy Blue

HOLYOKE SWEATER SCHEMATIC

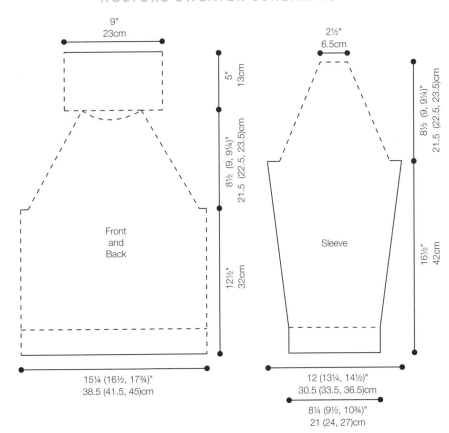

9"
23cm

5"
13cm

8½ (9, 9¼)"
21.5 (22.5, 23.5)cm

Front and Back

12½"
32cm

15¼ (16½, 17¾)"
38.5 (41.5, 45)cm

2½"
6.5cm

8½ (9, 9¼)"
21.5 (22.5, 23.5)cm

Sleeve

16½"
42cm

12 (13¼, 14½)"
30.5 (33.5, 36.5)cm

8¼ (9½, 10¾)"
21 (24, 27)cm

printmaker's pullover

page 32

The Printmaker's 2 x 2 rib grips you cozily from hem to neckline, pausing only for a few rows of stockinette at the sleeve cuff to let the fabric there roll back delightfully. The rib is slimming on the body; on the finished garment, it draws together the knitted material significantly. So don't be fooled by the pattern's negative ease—between the yarn and the rib, you'll slide right into this wear-anywhere pullover. Simultaneously worked raglan shaping and unobtrusive short rows that lift the back neck are key Twinkle tailoring tricks that are featured in many of the patterns; add them to your repertoire for your own designs.

SIZES
S (M, L)

Remember to use this guide to find your size based on your bust measurement: S = 34"–36" (86cm–91cm); M = 37"–39" (94cm–99cm); L = 40"–42" (102cm–107cm).

KNITTED MEASUREMENTS
Bust: 24 (26$\frac{1}{2}$, 29)" (61 [67, 73]cm)

Back length (not including collar): 23$\frac{1}{4}$ (24, 24$\frac{3}{4}$)" (58.5 [60.5, 62.5]cm)

MATERIALS
4 (4, 5) hanks Twinkle Handknits Soft Chunky, 100% virgin merino wool, 7 oz/200g, 83 yds/75m, #09 Black (A); 1 skein in #19 Cream (B) ⑥

US size 19 (15mm) 29" (75cm) and 24" (60cm) circular needles or size needed to obtain gauge

Stitch holders

Stitch markers

Tapestry needle

GAUGE
10 stitches and 14$\frac{1}{4}$ rows = 6" (15cm) in K2, P2 Rib on size 19 (15mm) needles.

Take the time to check your gauge.

NOTES
First, the sleeves are worked back and forth on a circular needle, then the body is worked in the round. The sleeves are joined to the body at the underarm and the sweater is knit in one piece from that point; change to a shorter circular needle when it is comfortable to do so. The front neck drop is formed by short rows. These short rows are counted like full rows when you are determining where to make decreases for raglan shaping. Mark the beginning of the round with a stitch marker in a color different from the others.

Twinkle Knit Bit
Avoid quitting knitting mid-row—work stretched between two needles is bound to pull stitches from at least one needle. To interrupt work, slip stitches from the needle holding fewer to the one holding more. It doesn't matter which stitches get slipped because the working yarn indicates where you have left off. Just slide the stitches back to the original needle to begin work again.

SLEEVES (MAKE 2)

With longer needle and A, cable cast on 17 (21, 21) stitches.

ROW 1 (RS): With A, knit.
ROW 2: With A, purl.
ROW 3: With B, knit.
ROW 4: With B, purl.
ROWS 5-8: Repeat Rows 1–4. Cut B.
ROWS 9-10: Repeat Rows 1–2.
ROW 11: *P2, k2; repeat from * to last stitch, p1.
ROW 12: K1, *p2, k2; repeat from * to end.

Continue in rib as established until Sleeve measures 19¼" (48.5cm) from the beginning, ending with a wrong-side row.

UNDERARM SHAPING

Bind off 2 (3, 2) stitches at the beginning of the next row and 1 (2, 1) stitches at the beginning of the following row. Place remaining 14 (16, 18) stitches on holder.

BODY

With longer needle, cast on 20 (22, 24) Front stitches, place marker to indicate right underarm, cast on 20 (22, 24) Back stitches, place marker to indicate left underarm and beginning of round—40 (44, 48) stitches. Join, being careful not to twist stitches.

ESTABLISH RIB

P1, *k2, p2; repeat from * to last 3 stitches, k2, p1.

Continue in rib as established until Body measures 14¾" (37cm) from the beginning, ending last round 1 (2, 1) stitch(s) before the end of round.

DIVIDE BODY

NEXT RND: Removing markers, bind off 2 (4, 2) stitches, work to 1 (2, 1) stitch(es) before marker, bind off 2 (4, 2) stitches, work to end of round—18 (18, 22) stitches each for Front and Back.

JOIN SLEEVES AND BODY

NEXT RND: Maintaining rib as established, work 14 (16, 18) Left Sleeve stitches, place marker to indicate raglan shaping, work 9 (9, 11) left Front stitches, place marker to indicate center Front, work 9 (9, 11) right Front stitches, place marker to indicate raglan shaping, work 14 (16, 18) Right Sleeve stitches, place marker to indicate raglan shaping, work 18 (18, 22) Back stitches, place marker to indicate raglan shaping and beginning of round—64 (68, 80) stitches.

NEXT 2 RNDS: *K1, work in rib to 1 stitch before next shaping marker, k1, slip marker; repeat from * around.

NECK AND RAGLAN SHAPING

NOTE: READ ALL SHAPING INSTRUCTIONS BEFORE BEGINNING.

NEXT RND (DEC RND): *Ssk, work to 2 stitches before shaping marker, k2tog, slip marker; repeat from * around—56 (64, 72) stitches.

Maintaining established pattern, repeat Dec Rnd every 4 rounds 4 times more.

SIZE M ONLY

Work 1 round even. Dec on Sleeves only once.

SIZE L ONLY

(Work 1 round even. Repeat Dec Rnd) 2 times.

ALL SIZES

AT THE SAME TIME, when 15 rounds of raglan shaping are complete, work short rows as follows, maintaining raglan shaping:

*Work to 2 stitches from center Front, wrap and turn (see page 152); repeat from * once.

**Work to 4 stitches from center Front, wrap and turn; repeat from ** once.

Continue on all stitches, picking up all wraps (see page 00).

ALL SIZES

24 stitches remain when all shaping is complete.

COLLAR

Work 16 rounds even in rib as established. Bind off very loosely in rib.

FINISHING

Sew sleeve and underarm seams. Weave in ends.

PRINTMAKER'S PULLOVER SCHEMATIC

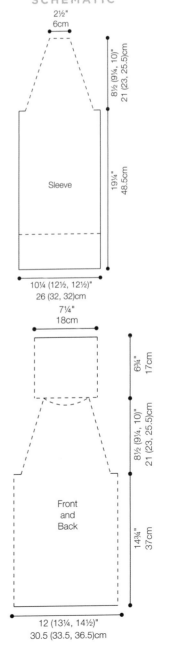

2½"
6cm

8½ (9¼, 10)"
21 (23, 25.5)cm

19¼"
48.5cm

Sleeve

10¼ (12½, 12½)"
26 (32, 32)cm

7¼"
18cm

6¾"
17cm

8½ (9¼, 10)"
21 (23, 25.5)cm

Front
and
Back

14¾"
37cm

12 (13¼, 14½)"
30.5 (33.5, 36.5)cm

nantucket cardigan

page 34

Stately pairs of cables define this distinctive cardigan as they emerge from the wide ribbed hem and ascend the background fabric of reverse stockinette, traveling the full front of the Nantucket Cardigan. As they climb, the cables play up the cardi's willowy shape. As you knit them, remember that some cable stitches on the outside edges will be absorbed by the underarm shaping; don't worry if you lack some of the stitches needed for a row of a cable pattern—just work the stitches you do have.

SIZES

XS (S, M, L)

Remember to use this guide to find your size based on your bust measurement: XS = 31"–33" (79cm–84cm); S = 34"–36" (86cm–91cm); M = 37"–39" (94cm–99cm); L = 40"–42" (102cm–107cm).

KNITTED MEASUREMENTS

Bust (buttoned): 33³/₄ (36¹/₂, 38³/₄, 41³/₄)" (85.5 [92, 98, 105.5]cm)

Back length (not including collar): 29 (29, 29³/₄, 30³/₄)" (73.5 [73.5, 75.5, 78]cm)

MATERIALS

5 (6, 6, 7) hanks Twinkle Handknits Soft Chunky, 100% virgin merino wool, 7 oz/200g, 83 yds/75m, #27 Urchin 🄶

US size 17 (12.75mm) 29" (75cm) circular needle

US size 19 (15mm) 29" (75cm) circular needle or size needed to obtain gauge

Cable needle

Stitch holders

Stitch markers

Tapestry needle

Six 1⁵/₈" (4cm) buttons

GAUGE

11 stitches and 16¹/₂ rows = 7" (18cm) in reverse stockinette stitch on size 19 (15mm) needle.

Take the time to check your gauge.

ABBREVIATIONS

Inc 1 (increase 1): Maintaining pattern, knit (or purl) 1 into right loop of stitch in row below next stitch on left-hand needle, then knit (or purl) the next stitch on left-hand needle.
T3R (twist 3 right): Slip next stitch onto cable needle and hold in back, k2, p1 from cable needle.
T3L (twist 3 left): Slip next 2 stitches onto cable needle and hold in front, p1, k2 from cable needle.

NOTES

The sleeves and body are knit back and forth; a circular needle is used to accommodate the many stitches. The fronts are worked without shoulder shaping, throwing the shoulder seam to the back. When working front Cable Stitch Patterns in sizes XS and S, the stitches closest to the underarm marker will disappear into the underarm shaping. Ignore these stitches on the Left

Front and Right Front Cable Stitch Pattern Charts as needed. Work cables only when there are enough stitches to do so. When a cable cannot be turned, work the "cable" stitches in stockinette stitch.

BODY

With smaller needle, and using long-tail cast-on, cast on 12 (13, 14, 15) stitches, place marker to indicate right underarm, cast on 28 (30, 32, 34) stitches, place marker to indicate left underarm, cast on 12 (13, 14, 15) stitches—52 (56, 60, 64) stitches.

Work 12 rows in k1, p1 rib (see page 150).

Change to larger needle and reverse stockinette stitch (see page 150).

ROW 1 (RS): Work Row 1 of Right Front Cable across next 12 stitches, purl to 0 (1, 2, 3) stitches beyond 2nd marker, work Row 1 of Left Front Cable across next 12 stitches.
ROW 2: Work even in patterns as established.
ROW 3 (DEC ROW): *Work in pattern to 3 stitches before marker, ssp, p1, slip marker, p1, p2tog; repeat from *, purl to end—50 (54, 58, 62) stitches.
ROWS 4–14: Work even.

ROW 15: Repeat Dec Row—48 (52, 56, 60) stitches.
ROWS 16–26: Work even.
ROW 27 (INC ROW): *Work in pattern to 1 stitch before marker, inc 1, slip marker, p1, inc 1; work to 2 stitches before next marker, inc 1, p1, slip marker, inc 1, work in pattern to end—50 (54, 58, 62) stitches.
ROWS 28–32: Work even.
ROW 33: Repeat Inc Row—52 (56, 60, 64) stitches.
ROWS 34–38: Work even.

Body measures approximately 21" (53.5cm) from the beginning. Place marker at each edge of the fabric to indicate the beginning of the front neck shaping.

DIVIDE BODY
ROW 1 (RS): P1, p2tog, work to 3 stitches before marker, ssp, p1; place these 10 (11, 12, 13) Right Front stitches on holder; remove marker, p1, p2tog, purl to 3 stitches before marker, ssp, p1; place these 26 (28, 30, 32) Back stitches on holder; remove marker, p1, p2tog, work to last 3 stitches, ssp, p1—10 (11, 12, 13) stitches remain for Left Front.

LEFT FRONT
ROW 2 AND ALL WS ROWS: Work even in pattern as established.
ROWS 3 AND 5: P1, p2tog, work to end.

Work Left Front Shaping Table through Row 15.

ALL SIZES: 5 (6, 7, 8) stitches remain when all shaping is complete.

ROWS 16–18 (18, 20, 22): Work even. Bind off.

BACK
Place Back stitches on needle. With wrong side facing, knit 1 row.

NEXT ROW (RS DEC ROW): P1, p2tog, purl to last 3 stitches, ssp, p1.

Repeat RS Dec Row every other row twice more—20 (22, 24, 26) stitches.

Work even until armhole measures 5½ (5½, 6½, 7¼)" (14 [14, 16.5, 18]cm), ending with a wrong-side row.

BACK SHOULDER SHAPING
NEXT ROW (RS): Work RS Dec Row—18 (20, 22, 24) stitches.

NEXT ROW (WS DEC ROW): K1, ssk, knit to last 3 stitches, k2tog, k1—16 (18, 20, 22) stitches.

Continue to decrease 1 stitch at each side on the next 4 rows—8 (10, 12, 14) stitches remain.

		XS, S	M	L
		LEFT FRONT SHAPING TABLE		
ROW 7		P1, p2tog, work to last 3 stitches, ssp, p1	P1, p2tog, work to last 3 stitches, ssp, p1	P1, p2tog, work to end
ROW 9		Work even	Work even	Work to last 3 stitches, ssp, p1
ROW 11		Work even	Work even	Work even
ROW 13		Work to last 3 stitches, ssp, p1	Work even	Work even
ROW 15		Work even	Work to last 3 stitches, ssp, p1	Work to last 3 stitches, ssp, p1

RIGHT FRONT SHAPING TABLE

	XS and S	M	L
Row 6	P1, p2tog, work to last 3 stitches, ssp, p1.	P1, p2tog, work to last 3 stitches, ssp, p1.	Work to last 3 stitches, ssp, p1.
Row 8	Work even.	Work even.	P1, p2tog, work to end.
Row 10	Work even.	Work even.	Work even.
Row 12	P1, p2tog, work to end.	Work even.	Work even.
Row 14	Work even.	P1, p2tog, work to end.	P1, p2tog, work to end.

Place back neck stitches on holder.

RIGHT FRONT
Place 10 (11, 12, 13) Right Front stitches on needle, with wrong side facing.

ROW 1 AND ALL WS ROWS: Work even in pattern as established.
ROWS 2 AND 4: Work to last 3 stitches, ssp, p1.

Work Right Front Shaping Table through Row 14.

ALL SIZES: 5 (6, 7, 8) stitches remain when all shaping is complete.

ROWS 15–18 (18, 20, 22): Work even. Bind off.

SLEEVES (MAKE 2)
With smaller needle, long-tail cast on 13 (13, 15, 17) stitches.

ROW 1 (RS): K1, *p1, k1; repeat from * to end.

Continue in rib as established for 11 more rows.

Change to larger needle and reverse stockinette stitch.

Work 14 rows even, ending with a wrong side row.

NEXT ROW (INC ROW): P1, inc 1, purl to last 2 stitches, inc 1, p1—15 (15, 17, 19) stitches.

Repeat Inc Row every 14 (12, 12, 12) rows 1 (2, 2, 2) times more—17 (19, 21, 23) stitches.

Work even until the sleeve measures approximately 21¼" (54cm), ending with a wrong-side row.

NEXT ROW (DEC ROW): P1, p2tog, purl to last 3 stitches, ssp, p1—15 (17, 19, 21) stitches.

SIZE XS ONLY: Repeat Dec Row every other row once, every 4 rows once, then every other row twice.

SIZES S, M AND L: Repeat Dec Row every other row 5 times.

ALL SIZES: 7 (7, 9, 11) stitches remain when shaping is complete.

FINISHING
Sew bound-off edge of Front shoulders to back Shoulder shaping.

NECK/FRONT BANDS
With right side facing and using smaller needle, pick up and knit 39 stitches along Right Front edge to neck shaping marker, place marker, pick up and knit 15 (15, 16, 17) stitches to shoulder seam, knit across 8 (10, 12, 14) Back neck stitches, pick up and knit 15 (15, 16, 17) stitches to neck shaping marker, place marker, pick up and knit 39 stitches along Left Front edge—116 (118, 122, 126) stitches.

ROW 1 (WS): *P1, k1; repeat from * to end.
ROW 2 (BUTTONHOLE ROW): P1, k1, *yo, k2tog, [p1, k1] twice, p1, yo, p2tog **, [k1, p1] 2 times, k1; repeat from * once and from * to ** once, continue in rib as established to end of row.

Work 4 rows even in k1, p1 rib. Bind off.

Sew in sleeves, easing in cap fullness. Sew sleeve seams. Weave in ends. Sew on buttons, creating shanks if necessary to accommodate the thickness of the knit fabric

NANTUCKET CARDIGAN CABLE STITCH PATTERN

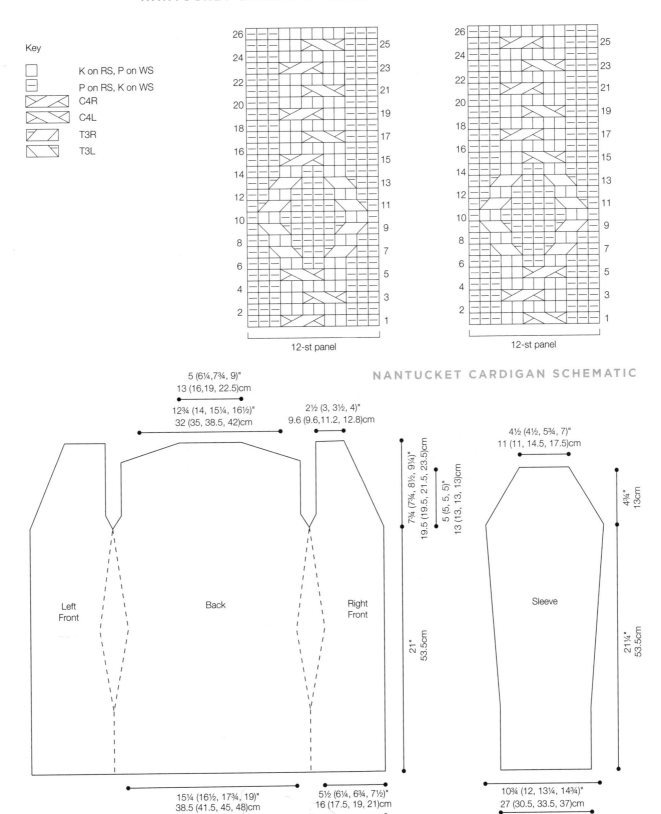

NANTUCKET CARDIGAN SCHEMATIC

LOST RESORTS

Thirty Songs for Thirty Knits

Vacation is usually a time to leave those earbuds and headphones behind—you want to absorb the sounds around you, not block them out. Still, there are moments when you might want a little soundtrack to your adventures, or even to close your eyes and listen to someone read you a recorded book or guide you through some language instruction. Riding to the airport or waiting to check your luggage, for example, are ideal opportunities to listen to that purchased music you just haven't had time to enjoy. So leave a little time to pack a player and CDs or download some files.

One option is to pick music suited to your destination or activities. A bachelorette on your last solo trip to Paris? Perhaps Françoise Hardy's *The Vogue Years* or one of the Hôtel Costes CDs are in order. Jetting to Seville for flamenco lessons? How about *Fantasía Flamenca* by Paco de Lucia or *La Leyenda del Tiempo* by El Camarón de la Isla? Travel is all about seeing things with fresh eyes, though, so when choosing music to bring on your Twinkle holiday, consider some favorite tunes covered by other artists. Last Town Chorus's languid, chic version of Bowie's "Modern Love," for instance, and Rickie Lee Jones' soulful rendition of "My Funny Valentine" illuminate the timeless appeal of those songs. The following is a possible score for your vacation. Listed within parentheses is the artist or musical group who originally recorded the song .

Music for Towns

"Wicked Game" by Giant Drag (Chris Isaak)

"Baby Jane" by Belle & Sebastian (Chet Baker)

"Chelsea Hotel No. 2" by Rufus Wainwright (Leonard Cohen)

"Just Like Heaven" by Dinosaur Jr. (The Cure)

"This Charming Man" by Death Cab for Cutie (Morrissey)

"I Fought in a War" by Damien Rice (Belle & Sebastian)

"Never Let Me Down Again" by Smashing Pumpkins (Depeche Mode)

"This Must Be the Place (Naïve Melody)" by Exit Clov (Talking Heads)

"Use Me" by Grace Jones (Bill Withers)

"Diamond Dogs" by Beck (David Bowie)

Music for Country

"I See a Darkness" by Johnny Cash and Will Oldham (Bonnie "Prince" Billy)

"Suspicious Minds" by My Morning Jacket (Elvis Presley)

"Downbound Train" by The Cardigans (Bruce Springsteen)

"When U Were Mine" by Crooked Fingers (Prince)

"Trouble" by Kristen Hersh (Cat Stevens)

"Modern Love" by Last Town Chorus (David Bowie)

"King of the Road" by Teddy Thompson & Rufus Wainwright (Roger Miller)

"Jolene" by The White Stripes (Dolly Parton)

"Such Great Heights" by Iron & Wine (The Postal Service)

"Voices Carry" (Acoustic) by Aimee Mann ('Til Tuesday)

Music for Seasides

"Diamond Sea" by the Yeah Yeah Yeahs (Sonic Youth)

"Mad World" by Gary Jules with Michael Andrews (Tears for Fears)

"Brand New Love" by Superchunk (Sebadoh)

"My Funny Valentine" by Rickie Lee Jones (Rodgers & Hart)

"This Night Has Opened My Eyes" by Underwater (The Smiths)

"Hallelujah" by Jeff Buckley (Leonard Cohen)

"The Killing Moon" by Nouvelle Vague (Echo & The Bunnymen)

"Smells Like Teen Spirit" by Tori Amos (Nirvana)

"Kid" (Live) by The Pretenders (The Kinks)

"Sea of Love" by Cat Power (Phil Phillips)

Many hotels now provide in-room mini stereo systems, so you may want to invest in a cord to route music from your player through the stereo's speakers. If your player handles video, you may even want to load some television or movies onto it for playback on those nights when you're adjusting to time changes and awake while public places are closed, when local TV is lacking, when you're hotel-bound by weather or illness, or when you're stuck on the tarmac or in the airport.

monterey jazz sweater

page 38

The Monterey's alluring color scheme and simple ornamentation highlight the sleek cut of this sexy pullover. The bold rib along the V-neckline and the broad ribbed hem stand out dramatically against the reverse stockinette stitch background and hug the knit close to the body. The raglan shoulder construction shapes the upper body neatly, permitting ease of movement and focusing attention on the silhouette. It's a polished look that hints at an earlier era while looking wholly fresh. To live up to its mesmerizing potential, the Monterey Jazz calls for a snug fit, so don't fret when you see the small measurements of the finished pullover—just follow the size guide given below. And keep in mind that the downy, loosely spun yarn is soft enough to wear close to your skin.

SIZES
S (M, L)

Remember to use this guide to find your size based on your bust measurement: S = 34"–36" (86cm–91cm); M = 37"–39" (94cm–99cm); L = 40"–42" (102cm–107cm).

KNITTED MEASUREMENTS
Bust: 28 (30½, 33)" (71 [77, 83.5]cm)

Back length (not including neck band): 18 (18¾, 19½)" (45.5 [47.5, 49]cm)

MATERIALS
3 (3, 3) hanks Twinkle Handknits Soft Chunky, 100% virgin merino wool, 7 oz/200g, 83 yds/75m, #03 Crimson **6**

US size 17 (12.75mm) 24" (60cm) and 29" (75cm) circular needles

US size 19 (15mm) 29" (75cm) circular needle or size needed to obtain gauge

Stitch holders

Stitch markers

Cable needle

Tapestry needle

GAUGE
11 stitches and 16½ rows = 7" (18cm) in reverse stockinette stitch on size 19 needles.

Take the time to check your gauge.

ABBREVIATIONS
Dec 1 (decrease 1): Preceding marker, work ssp on right side and k2tog on wrong side; following marker, work p2tog on right side and ssk on wrong side.
Dec 2 (decrease 2): Preceding marker, work sssp on right side and k3tog on wrong side; following marker, work p3tog on right side and sssk on wrong side.
Inc 1 (increase 1): Maintaining pattern, knit (or purl) 1 into right loop of stitch in row below next stitch on left-hand needle, then knit (or purl) the next stitch on left-hand needle.
MB (make bobble): (K1, p1, k1) into next stitch, turn; p3, turn; k3tog.

NOTES
The sleeves are worked back and forth on a circular needle first, then the body is worked in the round. The sleeves are joined to the body at the underarm and the sweater is knit in one piece from that point. Mark the beginning of the round with a stitch marker in a color different from the others.

SLEEVES (MAKE 2)

With smaller needle, cable cast on 13 (17, 17) stitches very loosely.

ROW 1 (RS): K1, *p2, k2; repeat from *.

Continue in rib as established for 5 more rows.

Change to larger needles and reverse stockinette stitch (see page 150); work 8 (16, 8) rows even, ending with a wrong-side row.

NEXT ROW (INC ROW): P1, inc 1, purl to last stitch, inc 1, p1—15 (19, 29) stitches.
SIZES S AND L ONLY: Work 7 rows, then repeat Inc Row—17 (–, 21) stitches.
ALL SIZES: Work even until Sleeve measures 12½" (32cm) from the beginning, ending with a wrong-side row.

UNDERARM SHAPING

Bind off 2 stitches at the beginning of the next 2 rows. Place the remaining 13 (15, 17) stitches on holder.

BODY

With smaller 24" (60cm) needle, cast on 18 (20, 22) Front stitches, place marker to indicate right underarm, cast on 18 (20, 22) Back stitches, place marker to indicate left underarm and beginning of round—36 (40, 44) stitches. Join, being careful not to twist stitches.

Work 22 rounds in k2, p2 rib. Change to larger needle.

RND 1: P1, inc 1, p1 (2, 3), place marker to indicate beginning of stitch chart, work Rnd 1 of chart across next 12 stitches, place marker, p1 (2, 3), inc 1, p1, slip marker, p1, inc 1, purl to 2 stitches before marker, inc 1, p1— 40 (44, 48) stitches.
RNDS 2–6: Continuing in established pattern, work through Rnd 6 of chart. Cut yarn.

DIVIDE FOR NECK

NOTE: SWEATER IS WORKED BACK AND FORTH IN ROWS FROM THIS POINT. READ ALL SHAPING INSTRUCTIONS BEFORE BEGINNING.

ROW 7 (RS): Slip first 10 (11, 12) stitches to right-hand needle. Join yarn in next stitch (center Front) and continue with established pattern, *work to 2 stitches before underarm marker, inc 1, p1, slip marker, p1, inc 1; repeat from * once, work to center front, turn—44 (48, 52) stitches.
ROW 8: Work even, removing chart markers.
ROW 9: P1, dec 2, work in pattern to last 4 stitches, dec 2, p1—40 (44, 48) stitches.
ROWS 10–11: Work even.
ROW 12: K1, dec 2, work in pattern to last 4 stitches, dec 2, k1—36 (40, 44) stitches.

DIVIDE FOR BODY

ROW 1 (RS): *Purl to 2 stitches before underarm marker, bind off next 4 stitches; repeat from * once, purl to end.

JOIN SLEEVES AND BODY

ROW 2: K5 (6, 7) Left Front stitches, place marker to indicate raglan shaping, k13 (15, 17) Left Sleeve stitches, place marker to indicate raglan shaping, k18 (20, 22) Back stitches, place marker to indicate raglan shaping, k13 (15, 17) Right Sleeve stitches, place marker to indicate raglan shaping, k5 (6, 7) Right Front stitches—54 (62, 70) stitches.

NECK AND RAGLAN SHAPING

NOTE: READ ALL SHAPING INSTRUCTIONS BEFORE BEGINNING.

Decrease at neck edge and work raglan shaping on Fronts, Back, and Sleeves, placing decreases on both sides of markers as indicated in Neck and Raglan Shaping Table (page 112) and working even on rows where cells are empty.

RS ROWS, IF DECREASE PRECEDES A MARKER:
Ssp (or sssp), p1, slip marker.
RS ROWS, IF DECREASE FOLLOWS A MARKER:
Slip marker, p1, p2tog (or p3tog).
WS ROWS, IF DECREASE PRECEDES A MARKER:
K2tog (or k3tog), k1, slip marker.
WS ROWS, IF DECREASE FOLLOWS A MARKER:
Slip marker, k1, ssk (or sssk).

ALL SIZES: 22 (26, 30) stitches remain when all shaping is complete.

Cut yarn and leave stitches on needle.

NECK BAND

With right side facing and using smaller needle, beginning at center front neck, pick up and knit 44 (50, 56) stitches around neck, including stitches on holder.

Work 3 rows in k2, p2 rib. Bind off loosely in rib.

Overlap left front band with right front band and sew edges of band along neckline.

FINISHING

Sew sleeve and underarm seams. Weave in ends.

MONTEREY JAZZ SWEATER STITCH PATTERN

☐ K on RS, P on WS
⊟ P on RS, K on on WS
⬤ MB
⬒ C6L

12-st panel

NECK AND RAGLAN SHAPING TABLE

	S	M	L
ROW 3	Dec 2 at Neck	Dec 2 at Neck	Dec 2 at Neck
ROW 4	Dec 1 on Back, Front, and Sleeves		
ROW 5		Dec 1 on Back, Front, and Sleeves	
ROW 6	Dec 1 at Neck	Dec 1 at Neck	Dec 1 on Back, Front, and Sleeves; Dec 1 at Neck
ROW 7	Dec 1 on Back, Front, and Sleeves		
ROW 8		Dec 1 at Neck	Dec 1 at Neck
ROW 9	Bind off 5 Sleeve stitches at beginning of row	Dec 1 on Back, Front, and Sleeves	
ROW 10	Bind off 5 Sleeve stitches at beginning of row		Dec 1 at Neck
ROW 11	Skip to Neck Band	Bind off 6 Sleeve stitches at beginning of row	Dec 1 on Back, Front and Sleeves
ROW 12	--	Bind off 6 Sleeve stitches at beginning of row	
ROW 13	--	Skip to Neck Band	Bind off 7 Sleeve stitches at beginning of row
ROW 14	--	--	Bind off 7 Sleeve stitches at beginning of row

MONTEREY JAZZ SWEATER SCHEMATIC

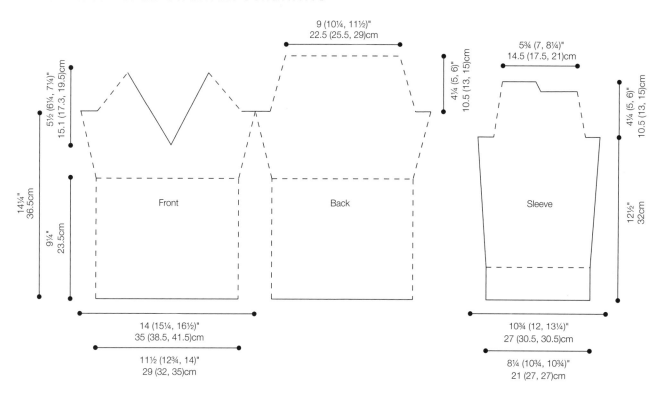

sirène du lac cardigan

page 39

In many ways, the Sirène du Lac is made like a woven cloth jacket: Front, back, sleeve, and collar pieces are shaped together, but instead of using darts and other tailoring methods to mold the fit, special knitting tricks sculpt the pieces. A textured stitch pattern takes the place of a textured weave. These understated details coalesce into a deceptively sophisticated, sleek, and useful knit garment. When shaping the body and sleeves, be sure to maintain the seed stitch pattern, working the increases—as knits or as purls—accordingly. Also, bind off the ribbed edge of the shawl collar loosely so it can stretch and roll smoothly.

SIZES
S (M, L)

Remember to use this guide to find your size based on your bust measurement: S = 34"–36" (86cm–91cm); M = 37"–39" (94cm–99cm); L = 40"–42" (102cm–107cm).

KNITTED MEASUREMENTS
Bust (buttoned): 34½ (36¾, 39¼)" (87 [93, 99]cm)

Back length (not including collar): 21¼ (21¾, 22½)" (53.5 [55, 57]cm)

MATERIALS
5 (6, 6) hanks Twinkle Handknits Soft Chunky, 100% virgin merino wool, 7 oz/200g, 83 yds/75m, #23 Haze **6**

US size 17 (12.75mm) 29" (75cm) circular needle

US size 19 (15mm) 29" (75cm) circular needle or size needed to obtain gauge

Stitch holders

Stitch markers

Coil-free safety pins or waste yarn for marker

Tapestry needle

Three 1⅝" (4cm) buttons

GAUGE
10 stitches and 17 rows = 6" (15cm) in seed stitch on size 19 (15mm) needle.

Take the time to check your gauge.

ABBREVIATIONS
Dec 1 (decrease 1): K2tog when the second stitch to be decreased is a knit stitch; p2tog when the second stitch to be decreased is a purl stitch.
Inc 1 (increase 1): Maintaining pattern, knit (or purl) 1 into right loop of stitch in row below next stitch on left-hand needle, then knit (or purl) the next stitch on left-hand needle.

Seed Stitch Pattern
ROW 1: *K1, p1; repeat from * across.
ROW 2: Purl the knit stitches, and knit the purl stitches.
Repeat Row 2 for pattern.

NOTES
The sleeves and body are all knit back and forth; a circular needle is used to accommodate the many stitches. When shaping, maintain Seed Stitch Pattern as established, working increases knitwise or purlwise as necessary.

POCKET LINING (MAKE 2)

With larger needle, and usng cable cast-on, cast on 9 (10, 10) stitches.

Work Seed Stitch Pattern for 10 rows.

Cut yarn and place stitches on holder.

BODY

With larger needle, cable cast on 13 (14, 15) stitches, place marker to indicate right underarm, cable cast on 28 (30, 32) stitches, place marker to indicate left underarm, cable cast on 13 (14, 15) stitches—54 (58, 62) stitches.

Work 10 rows in Seed Stitch Pattern, ending with a wrong-side row.

NEXT ROW (DEC ROW): *Work in pattern to 2 stitches before marker, dec 1, slip marker, dec 1; repeat from * once, work to end—50 (54, 58) stitches.

JOIN POCKETS

NEXT ROW (WS): Work 3 stitches, place next 9 (10, 10) stitches on holder, work in pattern across Pocket Lining stitches, work to last 12 (13, 13) stitches, place next 9 (10, 10) stitches on holder, work in pattern across Pocket Lining stitches, work remaining 3 stitches.
Work 8 rows even.
Repeat Dec Row—46 (50, 54) stitches.
Work 7 rows even. Place a safety pin on each Front edge to indicate the beginning of neck shaping.
NEXT ROW (RS): Dec 1, *work to 1 stitch before marker, inc 1, slip marker, inc 1; repeat from * once, work to last 2 stitches, dec 1—48 (52, 56) stitches.
Work 5 rows even.
NEXT ROW (RS): *Work to 1 stitch before marker, inc 1, slip marker, inc 1; repeat from * once, work to end—52 (56, 60) stitches.
NEXT ROW (WS): Dec 1, work to last

2 stitches, dec 1—50 (56, 58) stitches.

Work 4 rows even.

DIVIDE BODY

NEXT ROW (RS): Removing markers, work to 2 stitches before marker, place these 9 (10, 11) Right Front stitches on holder, bind off 4 stitches, work to 2 stitches before marker, place these 24 (26, 28) Back stitches on holder, bind off 4 stitches, work to end—9 (10, 11) Left Front stitches.

LEFT FRONT NECK, ARMHOLE, AND SHOULDER SHAPING

Work 1 row even.

NEXT ROW (RS): Dec 1, work to last 2 stitches, dec 1—7 (8, 9) stitches.
Work 1 row even.
NEXT ROW (RS): Dec 1, work to end—6 (7, 8) stitches.
Work 4 rows even.
NEXT ROW (WS): Dec 1, work to end—5 (6, 7) stitches.
Work 8 (10, 12) rows even.
NEXT ROW (RS): Bind off 2 (3, 3) stitches, work to end.

Work 1 row even.

Bind off remaining 3 (3, 4) stitches.

BACK ARMHOLE AND SHOULDER SHAPING

Place 24 (26, 28) Back stitches onto needle. With wrong side facing, work 1 row even.

*NEXT ROW (RS): Dec 1, work to last 2 stitches, dec 1—22 (24, 26) stitches.

Work 1 row even. Repeat from * once—20 (22, 24) stitches.

Work 12 (14, 16) rows even.

Bind off 2 (3, 3) stitches at the

beginning of the next 2 rows and 3 (3, 4) stitches at the beginning of the following 2 rows.

Put remaining 10 Back neck stitches on holder.

RIGHT FRONT NECK, ARMHOLE AND SHOULDER SHAPING

Place 9 (10, 11) Right Front stitches onto needle. With wrong side facing, work 1 row even.

NEXT ROW (RS): Dec 1, work to last 2 stitches, dec 1—7 (8, 9) stitches.
Work 1 row even.
NEXT ROW (RS): Work to last 2 stitches, dec 1—6 (7, 8) stitches.
Work 4 rows even.
NEXT ROW (WS): Work to last 2 stitches, dec 1—5 (6, 7) stitches.
Work 7 (9, 11) rows even.
NEXT ROW (WS): Bind off 2 (3, 3) stitches, work to end.

Work 1 row even.

Bind off remaining 3 (3, 4) stitches.

SLEEVES (MAKE 2)

With larger needle, cable cast on 15 (17, 19) stitches.

Begin Seed Stitch Pattern and work 12 rows even.

NEXT ROW (DEC ROW): Dec 1, work to last 2 stitches, dec 1—13 (15, 17) stitches.
Work 14 rows even.
NEXT ROW (INC ROW): Work 1 stitch, inc 1, work to last 2 stitches, inc 1, work last stitch—15 (17, 19) stitches.

Repeat Inc Row every 9 rows twice more—19 (21, 23) stitches.

Work 8 rows even.

SLEEVE CAP

Bind off 2 stitches at beginning of next 2 rows—15 (17, 19) stitches.

Work 0 (2, 2) rows even.

Work Dec Row on next row and then every other row 4 times more—5 (7, 9) stitches.

Work 1 (1, 3) rows even.

Bind off.

FINISHING

Sew Front and Back shoulders together.

NECK/FRONT BANDS

With right side facing and using smaller needle, pick up and knit 23 stitches along Right Front edge to neck shaping marker, place marker, pick up and knit 24 (26, 28) stitches to shoulder seam, knit across 10 Back neck stitches, pick up and knit 24 (26, 28) stitches to neck shaping marker, place marker, pick up and knit 23 stitches along Left Front edge—104 (108, 112) stitches.

ROW 1 (WS): P3, *k2, p2; repeat from *, ending last repeat with p3.
ROW 2: (BUTTONHOLE ROW): K1, *k2, p2, k2, yo, p2tog; repeat from * twice, work to end of row.

Work 1 more row in rib as established.

SHORT-ROW SHAPING

Work to 1 stitch before Left Front marker, wrap and turn (see Short Rows on page 152); work to 1 stitch before Right Front marker, wrap and turn. Work to 3 stitches before Left Front marker, wrap and turn; work to 3 stitches before Right Front marker, wrap and turn. Work to 5 stitches before Left Front marker, wrap and turn; work to 5 stitches before Right Front marker, wrap and turn. Continue to work 6 more short rows in this manner (each row being 2 stitches shorter than the previous row), the last being a wrong-side row ending 11 stitches before Right Front marker, turn.

NEXT ROW (RS): Work to end of row, picking up wraps.
NEXT ROW (WS): Work across all stitches, picking up wraps.

Bind off very loosely knitwise, using larger needle if necessary.

POCKET BANDS

Put 9 (10, 10) pocket stitches onto smaller needle.

Beginning with right side facing, work k1, p1 rib (see page 150) for 4 rows.

Bind off very loosely knitwise.

Repeat for second pocket.

Sew in sleeves. Sew sleeve seams. Sew pocket linings to wrong side of Fronts. Weave in ends. Sew on buttons, creating shanks if necessary to accommodate the thickness of the knit fabric.

SIRÈNE DU LAC CARDIGAN SCHEMATIC

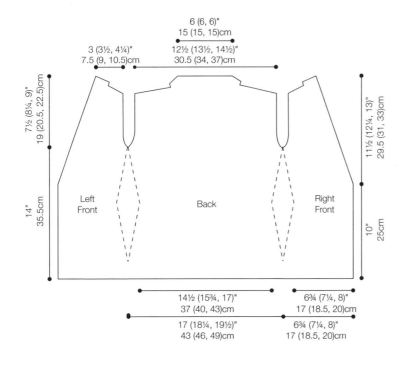

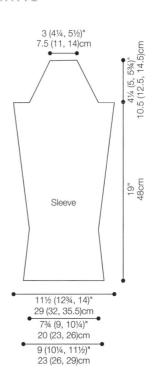

copenhagen hooded dress

page 39

The beguiling Copenhagen is worked in doubled-up mohair yarn on a circular needle. Then, double-pointed needles handle the stitch turns for the joined overlaps that form the flirty pleats along the bottom of the dress. When undoing the dropped stitch ladders that adorn the elbows, work slowly—mohair yarn's fuzzy fibers tend to cling to one another. Simple shaping techniques give the Copenhagen a surprisingly rectilinear outline when laid flat. The soft drape of the knitted mohair fabric, though, allows the dress to settle on the body in delicate, organic folds.

SIZES

XS (S, M, L)

Remember to use this guide to find your size based on your bust measurement: XS = 31"–33" (79cm–84cm); S = 34"–36" (86cm–91cm); M = 37"–39" (94cm–99cm); L = 40"–42" (102cm–107cm).

KNITTED MEASUREMENTS

Bust: 33¼ (36½, 38, 40½)" (84 [92.5, 96, 102.5]cm)

Back length (not including hood): 31¾ (32, 32¼, 32½)" (80.5 [81, 81.5, 82]cm)

MATERIALS

6 (7, 7, 8) balls of Twinkle Handknits Kids Mohair, 40% wool/35% mohair/25% acrylic 1¾ oz/50g, 310 yds/283m), #05 Silver Lavender ⑥

US size 11 (8mm) 29" (75cm) circular needle

US size 15 (10mm) 29" (75cm) circular needle or size needed to obtain gauge

Two US size 15 (10mm) double-pointed needles

Size 7 (4.5mm) crochet hook

Stitch holders

Stitch markers

Tapestry needle

GAUGE

10 stitches and 13 rows = 4" (10cm) in both reverse stockinette and Seed Stitch with 2 strands held together on size 15 needle.

Take the time to check your gauge.

ABBREVIATIONS

Dec 1 (decrease 1): K2tog when the second stitch to be decreased is a knit stitch; p2tog when the second stitch to be decreased is a purl stitch.

N1, N2, N3: Needle 1, needle 2, needle 3

Seed Stitch Pattern

RND 1: P1, *k1, p1; repeat from * across.

RND 2: (and all subsequent rounds/rows) Purl the knit stitches and knit the purl stitches.

NOTES

Two strands of yarn are held together throughout. The body is worked in the round to the neck and armhole shaping, then it is divided and worked back and forth on circular needles. The sleeves are worked side to side (from cap to cuff), with shaping worked on cast-on and bind-off rows.

BODY

With larger needle and 2 strands held together, and using long-tail cast-on, cast on 300 stitches, place marker to indicate beginning of round. Join to work in the round, being careful not to twist stitches.

Beginning with a knit round, work 5 rounds in garter stitch (see page 150).

Change to reverse stockinette stitch (see page 150) and work even until piece measures 8¼" (21cm) from the beginning.

MAKE PLEATS

Slip next 10 stitches to one dpn [N1] and hold in back, slip next 10 stitches to another dpn [N2], pivot N2 clockwise so that wrong side is facing and hold in front of N1, then holding left needle [N3] parallel to and in front of and N2 and N1, (knit together next stitch from N3, N2, and N1) 10 times; repeat from ★ around—100 stitches.

SIZE XS ONLY: Begin Seed Stitch Pattern, decreasing 5 stitches evenly spaced around.
SIZES S, M AND L: Begin Seed Stitch Pattern, increasing – (1, 7, 13) stitches evenly spaced around.
ALL SIZES: 95 (101, 107, 113) stitches.

NEXT RND: Work 49 (51, 53, 55) Front stitches, place marker to indicate right underarm, work 46 (50, 54, 58) Back stitches.
Work 12 rounds even.
NEXT RND (DEC RND): ★Dec 1, work to 2 stitches before marker, dec 1, slip marker; repeat from ★ once—91 (97, 103, 109) stitches.

Repeat Dec Rnd every 10 rounds twice more—83 (89, 95, 101) stitches.

Work even until Body measures 14¾" (37cm) above pleats.

DIVIDE BODY

NEXT ROW (RS): Work 17 (18, 19, 20) Left Front stitches, place these stitches on holder, bind off next 9 stitches for Placket, work to underarm marker and place these 17 (18, 19, 20) Right Front stitches on holder, work across 40 (44, 48, 52) Back stitches.

BACK

Work even until armhole measures 9 (9¼, 9½, 9¾)" (22.5 [23, 24, 24.5]cm). Bind off.

LEFT FRONT

Place Left Front stitches on needle.

Beginning with wrong side facing, work 7 rows even.

NEXT ROW (DEC ROW): Work to last 2 stitches, dec 1—16 (17, 18, 19) stitches.

Repeat Dec Row every 6 rows twice more—14 (15, 16, 17) stitches.

Work even until Left Front measures same as Back. Bind off.

RIGHT FRONT

Place Right Front stitches on needle.

Beginning with wrong side facing, work 7 rows even.

NEXT ROW (DEC ROW): Dec 1, work to end—16 (17, 18, 19) stitches.

Repeat Dec Row every 6 rows twice more—14 (15, 16, 17) stitches.

Work even until Right Front measures same as Back. Bind off.

SLEEVES (MAKE 2)

With larger needle and 2 strands held together, and using cable cast-on, cast on 6 stitches.

ROW 1 (RS): Begin Seed Stitch Pattern.
ROWS 2: Work across all stitches in Seed Stitch Pattern as established, then turn and cable cast on 6 stitches at end of row—12 stitches.
ROW 3: Work in Seed Stitch Pattern as established to end.
ROW 4: Work across all stitches in Seed Stitch Pattern as established, then turn and cable cast on 21 stitches at end of row—33 stitches.
ROW 5: Beginning with a knit stitch, work in Seed Stitch Pattern to end.
ROW 6: Work 12 stitches, bind off next 3 stitches, work to end.
ROW 7: Work to bound-off stitches, cast on 1 stitch using backward loop (Ladder Stitch), work to end—31 stitches.

Work even in Seed Stitch Pattern as established until Sleeve measures 15 (15, 16, 16)" (38.5 [39, 41, 41.5]cm) from bound-off stitches, ending with a wrong-side row.

Next Row (RS): Bind off 17 stitches (1 stitch remains on right-hand needle), drop next stitch off left-hand needle (Ladder Stitch), ★slip stitch on right needle to left needle, k1; repeat from ★ 2 times, bind off 1 stitch, work to end—12 stitches.

Continuing in Seed Stitch Pattern, bind off 6 stitches at the beginning of the next 2 right-side rows—0 stitches remain.

Drop Ladder Stitch all the way down to the bound-off stitches on Row 6.

FINISHING

Sew 14 (15, 16, 17) Front and Back shoulder stitches together on each side.

HOOD

With right side facing, using larger needle and 2 strands held together, pick up and knit 23 stitches along Right Front placket edge, pick up and knit 6 (7, 8, 9) Back neck stitches, place marker, pick up and knit 6 (7, 8, 9) Back neck stitches, pick up and knit 23 stitches along Left Front Placket—58 (60, 62, 64) stitches.

Work 41 rows even in Seed Stitch, ending with a wrong-side row.

NEXT ROW (DEC ROW): Work to 2 stitches before marker, dec 1, slip marker, dec 1, work to end—56 (58, 60, 62) stitches.

Repeat Dec Row every other row 6 times more—44 (46, 48, 50) stitches.

Work 1 row even.

Place first 22 (23, 24, 25) stitches on smaller needle and using larger needle and holding stitches parallel with right sides together, work three-needle bind-off (see page 153) across all stitches.

RIBBING

With right side facing and using smaller needle, pick up and knit 91 stitches around Hood.

Work 4 rows k1, p1 rib (see page 150). Bind off.

Sew edges of ribbing to bound-off placket stitches, leaving center placket stitch open.

Sew wider end of Sleeves into armholes. Sew Sleeve seams.

With crochet hook and 2 strands held together, crochet two chains each 36" (91cm) long.

Mark 7th stitch from cuff edge on each sleeve; weave crochet chain in and out every 3 rows along this stitch. Gather wrist and tie chain into a bow. Weave in ends.

COPENHAGEN HOODED DRESS SCHEMATIC

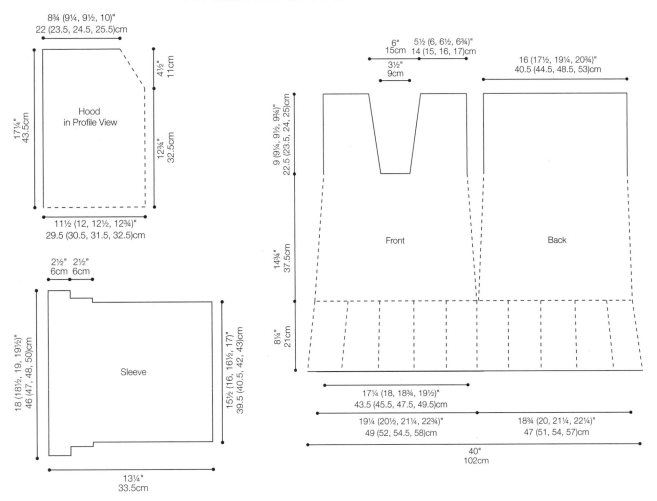

chesapeake charm school cardigan

page 40

The geometric shapes and crisp details of this short-sleeved cardigan evoke the clean lines of an earlier age—the Art Deco period, perhaps? Contributing to the precise silhouette are the cleverly built pleats, which mirror each other across the centers of the front and back of the upper body. Slipped onto double-pointed needles, trios of stitches are twisted to form folded pleats, a Twinkle design feat that results in nearly invisible joins. The pleats open when the Chesapeake is worn adding ample width for ease of movement and a comfortable fit despite the cardi's lean dimensions when laid flat.

SIZES

XS (S, M, L)

Remember to use this guide to find your size based on your bust measurement: XS = 31"–33" (79cm–84cm); S = 34"–36" (86cm–91cm); M = 37"–39" (94cm–99cm); L = 40"–42" (102cm–107cm).

KNITTED MEASUREMENTS

Bust (buttoned): 25 (26³/₄, 28, 30)" (63.5 [67.5, 71, 76]cm)

Back length: 18¹/₂ (19¹/₄, 20, 20¹/₂)" (46.5 [48.5, 51, 52]cm)

MATERIALS

4 (5, 5, 6) balls Twinkle Handknits Cruise, 70% silk/30% cotton, 1³/₄ oz/50g, 120 yds/109m, #08 White (A); 3 (3, 3, 3) skeins in #71 Peanut (B); and 3 (3, 3, 4) skeins in #67 Navy (C)

US size 15 (10mm) 29" (75cm) circular needle or size needed to obtain gauge

Three US size 15 (10mm) double-pointed needles (for pleats)

Stitch holders

Stitch markers

Tapestry needle

Four 1¹/₈" (3cm) buttons

GAUGE

10 stitches and 12¹/₂ rows = 4" (10cm) in stockinette stitch with four strands held together on size 15 needle.

Take the time to check your gauge.

ABBREVIATIONS

Sk2p: Slip 1, knit 2 together, pass slipped stitch over.
N1, N2, etc: Needle 1, needle 2, etc.
Dec 1 (decrease 1): On right side, ssk at beginning of row; k2tog at end of row; on wrong side, p2tog at beginning of row; ssp at end of row.

Double Pleats (worked over 19 stitches; 7 stitches remain when finished)
These pleats require three double-pointed needles (dpn) in addition to the main circular needle

Right-Folding Double Pleat
Slip next 4 stitches to one dpn [N1] and hold in back, slip next 3 stitches to another dpn [N2], pivot N2 counterclockwise so that stitches are with their wrong-side facing and hold in front of N1, slip next 6 stitches to another dpn [N3] and hold in front of N2; holding N3, N2, and N1 parallel to and behind left needle [N 4],

knit together next stitch from N2 and N1; (knit together next stitch from N3, N2, and N1) twice—1 stitch remains on N1, 0 stitches remain on N2, 4 stitches remain on N3.

Slip next 3 stitches from N4 to free dpn [N5], pivot N5 counterclockwise and hold in front of N3; holding N4, N5, N3, and N1 parallel, knit together next stitch from N5, N3, and N1; (knit together next stitch from N4, N5, and N3) twice; knit together next stitch from N4 and N3.

Left-Folding Double Pleat
Slip next 3 stitches to one dpn [N1] and hold in front, slip next 3 stitches to another dpn [N2], pivot N2 clockwise so that stitches on are with their wrong-side facing and hold behind N1, slip next 6 stitches to another dpn [N3] and hold behind N2; holding N1, N2, and N3 parallel to and in front of left needle [N4], knit together next stitch from N1 and N3; (knit together next stitch from N1, N2, and N3) twice—0 stitches remain on N1, 1 stitch remains on N2, 3 stitches remain on N3.

Slip next 3 stitches from N4 to free dpn [N5], pivot N5 clockwise and hold behind N3; holding N2, N3, N5, and N4 parallel, knit together next stitch from N2, N3, and N4; (knit together next stitch from N3, N5, and N4) twice; knit together next stitch from N5 and N4.

NOTES
Four strands of yarn are held together throughout. A circular needle is used to accommodate the many stitches. Keep front edge stitches in stockinette stitch throughout.

BODY
With 4 strands of C held together, and using long-tail cast-on, cast on 109 (113, 117, 121) stitches.

Beginning where indicated for size being worked, work Rows 1–12 of Stitch Pattern Chart (see page TK). Cut C. Attach B, and work Rows 13–24 of Stitch Pattern Chart. Cut B.

NEXT ROW (WS): With A, p27 (28, 29, 30) Left Front stitches, place marker to indicate underarm, p2tog, p53 (55, 57, 59) Back stitches, place marker to indicate underarm, p27 (28, 29, 30) Right Front stitches—108 (112, 116, 120) stitches.

Work 4 rows in Stockinette stitch (see page 150).

DIVIDE BODY
NEXT ROW (RS): Removing markers, knit to 2 stitches before marker, place these 25 (26, 27, 28) Right Front stitches on holder, bind off 4 stitches, knit to 2 stitches before marker, place these 50 (52, 54, 56) Back stitches on holder, bind off 4 stitches, knit across Left Front stitches to end—25 (26, 27, 28) stitches.

LEFT FRONT
ROWS 1 AND 3: Purl.
ROW 2 (DEC ROW): Dec 1, knit to end—24 (25, 26, 27) stitches.
ROW 4 (MAKE PLEATS): K2 (3, 3, 4), work Right-Folding Double Pleat over next 19 stitches, knit to end—12 (13, 14, 15) stitches remain.

Work 1 row even, then repeat Dec Row—11 (12, 13, 14) stitches remain.

SHAPE LEFT NECK
NEXT ROW (DEC ROW): Dec 1, purl to end.

Repeat Dec Row every other row 1 (3, 3, 4) times and then every 4 rows 1 (0, 0, 0) time—8 (8, 9, 9) stitches.

Work even until armhole measures 9 (9¾, 10½, 11)" (22.5 [24.5, 25.5, 28]cm).

Bind off.

BACK
Place 50 (52, 54, 56) Back stitches onto needle.

ROWS 1 AND 3 (WS): With A, purl.
ROW 2 (DEC ROW): Dec 1, knit to last 2 stitches, dec 1—48 (50, 52, 54) stitches.
ROW 4 (MAKE PLEATS): K1 (1, 2, 2), make Right-Folding Double Pleat over next 19 stitches, k8 (10, 10, 12), make Left-Folding Double Pleat over next 19 stitches, k1 (1, 2, 2)—24 (26, 28, 30) stitches remain.

Work even until armhole measures 6½ (7¼, 8, 8½)" (16.5 [18, 20, 21.5]cm) ending with a right-side row.

SHAPE SHOULDERS AND BACK NECK
NOTE: READ ALL SHAPING INSTRUCTIONS BEFORE BEGINNING.

ROWS 1–3: Dec 1, work to last 2 stitches, dec 1—18 (20, 22, 24) stitches.

ROW 4 (RS): Dec 1, k4 (5, 5, 6), join new yarn, bind off 6 (6, 8, 8) stitches, knit to last 2 stitches, dec 1—5 (6, 6, 7) stitches remain on each side.

Working both sides at once with separate balls of yarn, follow the Shoulder and Neck Shaping Table (page 121).

ALL SIZES: No stitches remain when all shaping is complete.

RIGHT FRONT
Place 25 (26, 27, 28) Right Front stitches onto needle.

ROWS 1 AND 3 (WS): With A, purl.
ROW 2 (DEC ROW): Knit to last 2 stitches, dec 1—24 (25, 26, 27) stitches.

SHOULDER AND NECK SHAPING TABLE

	XS	S	M	L
Row 5	Dec 1 at each armhole edge	Dec 1 at each armhole edge and at each neck edge	Dec 1 at each armhole edge and at each neck edge	Dec 1 at each armhole edge and at each neck edge
Row 6	Dec 1 at each armhole edge and at each neck edge	Dec 1 at each armhole edge	Dec 1 at each armhole edge	Dec 1 at each armhole edge and at each neck edge
Row 7	Dec 1 at each armhole edge	Dec 1 at each armhole edge and at each neck edge	Dec 1 at each armhole edge and at each neck edge	Dec 1 at each armhole edge and at each neck edge
Row 8	Dec 1 at each armhole edge	Dec 1 at each armhole edge	Dec 1 at each armhole edge	Dec 1 at each armhole edge

ROW 4 (MAKE PLEATS): K3 (3, 4, 4), work Left-Folding Double Pleat over next 19 stitches, knit to end—12 (13, 14, 15) stitches remain.

Work 1 row even, the repeat Dec Row—11 (12, 13, 14) stitches.

SHAPE RIGHT NECK
NEXT ROW (DEC ROW): Purl to last 2 stitches, dec 1—10 (11, 12, 13) stitches.

Repeat Dec Row every other row 1 (3, 3, 4) times and every 4 rows 1 (0, 0, 0) time—8 (8, 9, 9) stitches.

Work even until armhole measures same as for Left Front. Bind off.

SLEEVES (MAKE 2)
With 4 strands of A held together, cast on 23 (25, 27, 29) stitches.

ROW 1 (RS): K1, *p1, k1; repeat from * across.
Work 7 more rows in k1, p1 rib as established.
ROW 9: K9 (10, 11, 13), *M1, k1; repeat from * 3 times, M1, k10 (11, 12, 12)—28 (30, 32, 34) stitches.
ROW 10: P13 (12, 13, 14), *M1-p, p1 (2, 2, 2); repeat from * 3 times, p11

(10, 11, 12)—32 (34, 36, 38) stitches.

UNDERARM SHAPING
ALL SIZES: Continuing in stockinette stitch, bind off 2 stitches at the beginning of the next 2 rows—28 (30, 32, 34) stitches.

CAP SHAPING
NEXT ROW (DEC ROW): Dec 1, work to last 2 stitches, dec 1.

Continuing in stockinette stitch, repeat Dec Row every 3 (4, 3, 4) rows 3 (2, 3, 3) times more and every 0 (3, 4, 3) rows once.

Bind off remaining 20 (22, 22, 24) stitches.

FINISHING
BUTTON BAND
With right side facing and 4 strands held together, pick up and knit 28 stitches along Right Front edge.

Work 3 rows in k1, p1 rib. Bind off.

BUTTONHOLE BAND
With right side facing and 4 strands held together, pick up and knit 28 stitches along Left Front edge.

ROW 1 (WS): *K1, p1; repeat from * across.
ROW 2 (BUTTONHOLE ROW): K1, p1, k1, yo, k2tog, p1, (k1, p1) 3 times, yo, p2tog, k1, (p1, k1) 3 times, yo, k2tog, p1, (k1, p1) twice.
ROW 3: Repeat Row 1. Bind off.

Sew bound-off Front shoulder stitches to shaped Back shoulders.

NECK BAND
With right side facing and 4 strands held together, pick up and knit 3 stitches along top of Buttonhole Band, 16 (18, 19, 20) stitches up Left Front neckline, 20 (20, 22, 22) stitches along Back neck, 16 (18, 19 20) stitches down Right Front neckline, and 3 stitches along top of Button Band—58 (62, 68, 70) stitches.

ROW 1 (WS): *K1, p1; repeat from * across.
ROW 2 (BUTTONHOLE ROW): K1, p1, yo, p2tog, continue in rib as established.
ROW 3: Repeat Row 1. Bind off.

Sew sleeve and underarm seams. Weave in ends. Sew buttons onto Left Front opposite buttonholes.

Twinkle Knit Bit

When using double-pointed needles (dpns), it can be difficult to keep track of how you've numbered them. One system is to draw, with a permanent marker, rings around the barrels of the needles, where the number of rings corresponds to the needle number. For example, two rings marked near the end of a dpn indicates needle #2. Coat the rings with clear nail polish to preserve them. Leave the spare needle unmarked so it can fill in for a lost needle of any given number. For less a permanent means of marking needles, twist colored rubber bands around dpns to differentiate them, or cap them with point protectors.

Key

☐ K on RS, P on WS
⊟ P on RS, K on WS
◿ SSK
◎ YO
◹ K2tog
⧄ SK2P

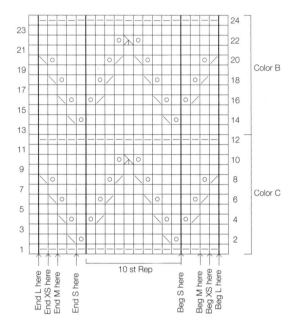

Work edge stiches in stockinette st, then beg when indicated on chart for size being worked. Omit yarn over at edges if you cannot work accompanying decrease.

CHESAPEAKE CHARM SCHOOL CARDIGAN SCHEMATIC

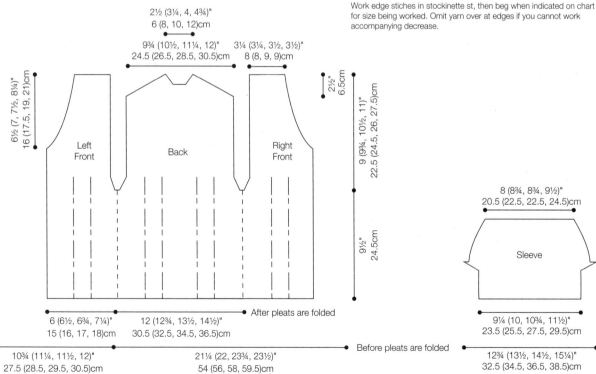

big sur cardigan

page 40

This elegant cardigan can do double-duty as an accessory to set off the rest of an outfit. The pattern's pliable silk-and-cotton blend yarn, knitted with four strands held as one, has the resilience and sturdiness to let the lacework drape elegantly over the body while keeping its shape. To knit the Big Sur, you'll first work the body and sleeves back and forth, then pick up the sleeves at the underarm and work the cardi as a whole the rest of the way. Decreases shape the raglan shoulder, and short rows on the cardigan's fronts shape the neck. When sewing on the pockets, you may want to use safety pins to situate the stitches as needed to shape the charming, purse-like contours seen in the photos.

SIZES

XS (S, M, L)

Remember to use this guide to find your size based on your bust measurement: XS = 31"–33" (79cm–84cm); S = 34"–36" (86cm–91cm); M = 37"–39" (94cm–99cm); L = 40"–42" (102cm–107cm).

Bust (buttoned): 27$\frac{1}{2}$ (30$\frac{1}{4}$, 33, 35$\frac{3}{4}$)" (69.5 [77, 83.5, 90]cm)

Back length: 14$\frac{3}{4}$ (14$\frac{3}{4}$, 15$\frac{1}{4}$, 15$\frac{1}{4}$)" (37 [37, 38.5, 38.5]cm)

MATERIALS

3.5 × 120 = 420 yds

10 (11, 12, 14) balls Twinkle Handknits Cruise, 70% silk/30% cotton, 1$\frac{3}{4}$ oz/50g, 120 yds/109m, #08 White ②

US size 13 (9mm) 29" (75cm) circular needle

US size 15 (10mm) 29" (75cm) circular needle or size needed to obtain gauge

Stitch holders

Stitch markers

Tapestry needle

Five 1" (2.5cm) buttons

GAUGE

11 stitches and 18$\frac{1}{2}$ rows = 5" (12.5cm) in Lace Pattern with 4 strands held together on size 15 (10mm) needle.

Take time to check your gauge.

ABBREVIATION

Sssk (slip, slip, slip, knit): Slip next 3 stitches one at a time as if to knit, insert left-hand needle into all 3 stitches, and knit them together—creates a left-leaning double decrease.

Lace Pattern (multiple of 6 + 2; see chart, page 26)
ROW 1 (RS): K1, *yo, sssk, yo, k3; repeat from * across, k1.
ROW 2: **Purl.**
ROW 3: K1, *k3; yo, sssk, yo; repeat from * across, k1.
ROW 4: **Purl.**
Repeat Rows 1–4 for pattern.

The sleeves and body are both knit back and forth; a circular needle is used to accommodate the many stitches. Sleeves are joined to the body at the underarm and the sweater is knit in one piece from that point. The front neck drop is formed by short rows. Four strands of yarn are held together throughout.

When working the lace pattern at the same time as you are decreasing for shaping, work the (yo, sssk, yo) of the lace pattern only when you have 3 stitches available for the complete double decrease; otherwise, work those stitches in stockinette stitch, eliminating both yarn overs and the decrease.

SLEEVES (MAKE 2)

With smaller needle and 4 strands held together, and usng cable cast-on, cast on 26 (26, 30, 30) stitches. Work 8 rows in k2, p2 rib (see page 150).

Change to larger needle and work 6 rows Lace Pattern.

UNDERARM SHAPING

Bind off 2 stitches at the beginning of the next 2 rows. Place the remaining 22 (22, 26, 26) stitches on holder.

BODY

With smaller needle and 4 strands held together, cable cast on 15 (17, 19, 21) stitches, place marker to indicate right underarm, cast on 38 (40, 42, 44) stitches, place marker to indicate left underarm, cast on 15 (17, 19, 21) stitches—68 (74, 80, 86) stitches.

Work 8 rows in k2, p2 rib. Change to larger needle.

Work 9 rows Lace Pattern.

NEXT ROW (DEC ROW): Work to 2 stitches before marker, *p2tog, slip marker, ssp; repeat from * once, then work to end—64 (70, 76, 82) stitches.

Repeat Dec Row every 4 rows twice more—56 (62, 68, 74) stitches.

Work even until Body measures 8¼" (21cm) from the beginning, ending with a wrong-side row.

DIVIDE BODY

NOTE: READ ALL SHAPING INSTRUCTIONS BEFORE BEGINNING.

ROW 1 (RS): *Work to 2 stitches before marker, bind off 4 stitches (removing marker); repeat from * once, work to end.

JOIN SLEEVES AND BODY

ROW 2: P10 (12, 14, 16) Left Front stitches, place marker to indicate raglan shaping, p22 (22, 26, 26) Left Sleeve stitches, place marker to indicate raglan shaping, p28 (30, 32, 34) Back stitches, place marker to indicate raglan shaping, p22 (22, 26, 26) Right Sleeve stitches, place marker to indicate raglan shaping, p10 (12, 14, 16) Right Front stitches—92 (98, 112, 118) stitches.

NECK AND RAGLAN SHAPING

Work raglan shaping on Fronts, Back, and Sleeves and short-row neck shaping, placing decreases on both sides of the marker as indicated in the Neck and Raglan Shaping Table (page 125) and working even on rows where cells are empty.

RAGLAN DECREASE PRECEDING MARKER: Work to 2 stitches before marker, ssp.

RAGLAN DECREASE FOLLOWING MARKER: Slip marker, p2tog.

FOR SHORT ROWS: Work until you reach indicated number of stitches from Front Edge, then wrap and turn (see Short Rows on page 152). When you see ** instead of a number for the size being worked, short-row shaping is complete for that size. At that point, put the 4 (5, 6, 7) stitches that are not being worked at the Front edges on holders or waste yarn and continue working even on shortened row until all shaping is complete.

ALL SIZES: 54 (58, 62, 66) stitches remain when all shaping is complete: [6 (7, 8, 9) Front stitches each side, 14 Sleeve stitches and 14 (16, 18, 20) Back stitches].
Cut yarn and leave remaining stitches on needle.

FINISHING
BUTTON BAND

With right side facing, using smaller needle and 4 strands held together, pick up and knit 30 stitches along left Front edge.

NEXT ROW (WS): P2, *k2, p2; repeat from * across.

Work 4 rows even in established rib. Bind off.

BUTTONHOLE BAND

With right side facing and using smaller needle and 4 strands held together, pick up and knit 30 stitches along right Front edge.

ROW 1 (WS): P2, *k2, p2; repeat from * across.
ROW 2 (BUTTONHOLE ROW): K2, p1, yo, k2tog, k1, p2, k2, yo, p2tog, k2, p2, yo, k2tog, p2, k2, p1, yo, k2tog, k1, p2, k2.

Work 3 rows even in rib as established. Bind off.

NECK AND RAGLAN SHAPING TABLE

Row #	Short Row (Right Front Edge)	Short Row (Left Front Edge)	XS	S	M	L
ROW 3 (RS)						
ROW 4			Back and Fronts	Back and Fronts	Back, Fronts, and Sleeves	Back, Fronts, and Sleeves
ROW 5						
ROW 6			Sleeves	Sleeves		
ROW 7						
ROW 8			Back and Fronts	Back and Fronts	Back, Fronts, and Sleeves	Back, Fronts, and Sleeves
ROW 9		2 (2, 2, 2)				
ROW 10	2 (2, 2, 2)					
ROW 11		3 (3, 3, 3)				
ROW 12	3 (3, 3, 3)		Back, Fronts, and Sleeves	Back, Fronts, and Sleeves	Back, Fronts, and Sleeves	Back, Fronts, and Sleeves
ROW 13		4 (4, 4, 4)				
ROW 14	4 (4, 4, 4)					
ROW 15		★★(5, 5, 5)				
ROW 16	★★ (5, 5, 5)		Back and Fronts	Back and Fronts	Back and Sleeves	Back, Fronts, and Sleeves
ROW 17		- (★★, 6, 6)				
ROW 18	- (★★, 6, 6)		Sleeves	Sleeves	Fronts	
ROW 19		- (-, ★★, 7)				
ROW 20	- (-, ★★, 7)		Back	Back and Fronts	Back and Sleeves	Back, Fronts, and Sleeves
ROW 21	--					
ROW 22			Sleeves and Back	Sleeves and Back	Back and Fronts	Back and Fronts
ROW 23						
ROW 24			Back	Back	Back, Fronts, and Sleeves	Back, Fronts, and Sleeves
ROW 25			Skip to Button Band	Skip to Button Band		
ROW 26	--	--				

NECK BAND

With right side facing and using smaller needle and 4 strands held together, pick up and knit 5 stitches from top of Buttonhole Band; knit 4 (5, 6, 7) short-row stitches from holder, picking up wraps, pick up and knit 6 (5, 4, 3) stitches along straight edge, k46 (48, 50, 52) stitches from needle; pick up and knit 6 (5, 4, 3) stitches along straight edge, k4 (5, 6, 7) short-row stitches from holder, pick up and knit 5 stitches from top of Button Band—76 (78, 80, 82) stitches.

Work 1 row in k2, p2 rib.

NEXT ROW (RS): Work 2 stitches, yo, k2tog (or p2tog) to maintain rib, continue in rib to end.

Work 3 rows even in rib as established. Bind off.

POCKETS (MAKE 2)

With larger needle, cable cast on 10 stitches.

ROW 1 (RS): Knit.

ROW 2: Cast on 3 stitches; purl across—13 stitches.

ROW 3: Cast on 3 stitches; k2, *yo, sssk, yo, k3; repeat from * to last 2 stitches, k2—16 stitches.

ROW 4: Cast on 2 stitches; purl across—18 stitches.

ROW 5: Cast on 2 stitches; work Row 1 of Lace Pattern—20 stitches.

Continue in Lace Pattern as established for 14 rows.

NEXT ROW (WS): (P2tog) across—10 stitches.

Work 4 rows in k2, p2 rib. Bind off.

Sew sleeve and underarm seams. Weave in ends. Sew pockets to Cardigan with ⅔ on Front and ⅓ on Back as indicated on schematic, easing in shaped lower edge to form rounded pouch. Sew buttons onto Left Front opposite buttonholes.

BIG SUR CARDIGAN LACE STITCH PATTERN

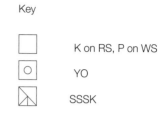

Key

☐ K on RS, P on WS

○ YO

◩ SSSK

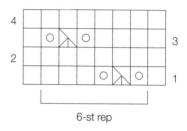

6-st rep

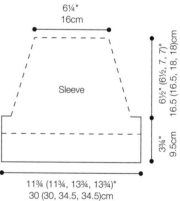

6¼"
16cm

Sleeve

6½" (6½, 7, 7)"
16.5 (16.5, 18, 18)cm

3¾"
9.5cm

11¾ (11¾, 13¾, 13¾)"
30 (30, 34.5, 34.5)cm

BIG SUR CARDIGAN SCHEMATIC

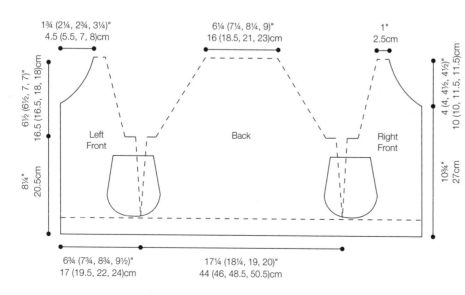

1¾ (2¼, 2¾, 3¼)"
4.5 (5.5, 7, 8)cm

6¼ (7¼, 8¼, 9)"
16 (18.5, 21, 23)cm

1"
2.5cm

6½ (6½, 7, 7)"
16.5 (16.5, 18, 18)cm

Left Front

Back

Right Front

4 (4, 4½, 4½)"
10 (10, 11.5, 11.5)cm

8¼"
20.5cm

10¾"
27cm

6¾ (7¾, 8¾, 9½)"
17 (19.5, 22, 24)cm

17¼ (18¼, 19, 20)"
44 (46, 48.5, 50.5)cm

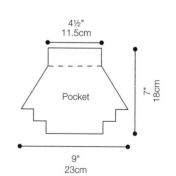

4½"
11.5cm

Pocket

7"
18cm

9"
23cm

pacifica jacket

page 42

The right- and left-slanting decreases and yarn overs in this lace pattern are simple stitches, but worked in the right combination and yarn, they create a stunning effect. The generous width provides enough knitted fabric for the gathered fronts to drape and swing prettily. A three-needle bind-off joins the tops of the front sections, forming a shawl collar that, when turned down, raises the front panels. Stitches along the bottom edge are picked up and crocheted to add the open loops. The sleeves are set into the body and their edges, like those of the bottom of the body, are kept in garter stitch for stability and ease of seaming.

SIZES
S (M, L)

Remember to use this guide to find your size based on your bust measurement: S = 34"–36" (86cm–91cm); M = 37"–39" (94cm–99cm); L = 40"–42" (102cm–107cm).

KNITTED MEASUREMENTS
Bust: 44½ (49, 53½)" (112.5 [124, 135.5]cm), including unturned-back shawl collar

Back length (including crocheted trim): 17½ (18¼, 19)" (44 [46, 48]cm)

MATERIALS
11 (11, 12) balls Twinkle Handknits Cruise, 70% silk/30% cotton, 1¾ oz/50g, 120 yds/109m, #34 Capri **2**

US size 17 (12.75mm) 29" (75cm) circular needle or size needed to obtain gauge; one extra size 17 (12.75mm) needle for three-needle bind-off

US size G/6 (4mm) crochet hook

Stitch holders

Stitch markers

Tapestry needle

GAUGES
10 stitches and 12½ rows = 4" (10cm) in stockinette stitch with 4 strands held together on size 17 (12.75mm) needles.

9-stitch repeat of lace pattern = 4½" (11cm)

Take the time to check your gauge.

ABBREVIATION
Inc 1 (increase 1): Maintaining pattern, knit (or purl) 1 into right loop of stitch in row below next on left-hand needle, then knit (or purl) the next stitch on left-hand needle.
ROW 1 (RS): *K1, yo, k2, ssk, k2tog, k2, yo; repeat from * to end.
ROW 2: Purl.
ROW 3: *Yo, k2, ssk, k2tog, k2, yo, k1; repeat from * to end.
ROW 4: Purl.
Repeat Rows 1–4 for pattern.

The body and sleeves are all knit back and forth, holding four strands of yarn throughout; a circular needle is used to accommodate the many stitches. The top edges of the fronts are joined together to form a shawl collar. Keep the front and armhole edge stitches in garter stitch throughout.

BODY

With 4 strands held together, and using cable cast-on, cast on 91 (100, 118) stitches.

ROW 1 (RS): K3, place marker, work Row 1 of Lace Pattern across next 27 (27, 36) stitches, place marker, k2, work Row 1 of Lace Pattern across next 27 (36, 36) stitches, place marker, k2, work Row 1 of Lace Pattern across next 27 (27, 36) stitches, place marker, k3.

ROW 2: K3, ★work Lace Pattern to marker, slip marker, k2, slip marker; repeat from ★ 2 times, k1.

Keeping the first and last 3 stitches, along with the 2 stitches between the lace panels, in garter stitch (knit every row), work three full repeats of the Lace Pattern, ending with a wrong side row.

DIVIDE BODY

NEXT ROW (RS): K3, work Lace Pattern across next 18 (18, 27) stitches, place marker, k2, place these 23 (23, 32) Right Front stitches on holder, bind off next 7 stitches (removing marker), k2, place marker, work to next marker, slip marker, k2, place these 31 (40, 40) Back stitches on holder, bind off next 7 stitches (removing marker), k2, place marker, work in pattern to end—23 (23, 32) Left Front stitches.

LEFT FRONT

Work even until Left Front measures 9 (10¼, 11½)" (22.5 [26, 29]cm)from underarm bind-off row. Place stitches on holder.

Place marker in fabric on armhole edge 3¼ (3¾, 3¾)" (8 [9.5, 9.5]cm) from top edge.

BACK

Place 31 (40, 40) Back stitches on needle. Beginning with a wrong-side row, work even until Back measures 7½ (8¼, 9)" (19 [20.5, 22.5]cm) from underarm bind-off row. Bind off.

RIGHT FRONT

Place 23 (23, 32) Right Front stitches on needle. Beginning with a wrong-side row, work even until Right Front measures 9 (10¼, 11½)" (22.5 [26, 29]cm) from underarm bind-off row, ending with a wrong-side row.

Place Left Front stitches on a needle.

Place marker in fabric on armhole edge 3¼ (3½, 3½)" (8 [9.5, 9.5]cm) from top edge.

Holding right side of Right Front together with right side of Left Front stitches, work three-needle bind-off (see page 153) across all stitches to form center back collar seam.

SLEEVES (MAKE 2)

With 4 strands held together, cable cast on 23 (25, 27) stitches.

ROW 1 (RS): K7 (8, 9), place marker, work Row 1 of Lace Pattern across next 9 stitches, place marker, k7 (8, 9).

Working in stockinette stitch on either side of lace panel, work 5 more rows even as established.

NEXT ROW (INC ROW): Maintaining pattern, work 1, inc 1, work to last stitch, inc 1, work 1—25 (27, 29) stitches.

Repeat Inc Row every 6 rows 3 times more—31 (33, 35) stitches.

Work even until Sleeve measures 10¼" (26cm) from the beginning, measured from cast-on row along stockinette stitch border, ending with a wrong-side row.

UNDERARM SHAPING

Bind off 4 stitches at the beginning of the next 2 rows—23 (25, 27) stitches.

CAP SHAPING

Continuing in pattern, work 2 rows even.

NEXT ROW (DEC ROW): K1, ssk, work to last 3 stitches, k2tog, k1—21 (23, 25) stitches.

Repeat Dec Row every 4 rows 2 (3, 2) times, every 6 rows 0 (0, 1) time, then every other row 2 (1, 1) time(s)—13 (15, 17) stitches.

Work 1 row even. Bind off.

CROCHET BORDER

With right side facing and using crochet hook, join yarn at lower Left Front edge.

Work Row 1 into cast-on stitches or yarn-over spaces.

ROW 1 (RS):
SIZE S ONLY: Ch 3 (counts as dc and ch 2), dc in same stitch as joining stitch, ★ch 3, skip 2 stitches, (dc, ch 2, dc) in next stitch, ch 3, skip 1 stitch, (dc, ch 2, dc) in next stitch; repeat from ★ 17 times, turn.

SIZE M AND L ONLY: Ch 3 (counts as dc), dc in same stitch, *ch 3, skip 2 stitches, (dc, ch 2, dc) in next stitch * – (8, 24) times, *ch 3, skip 2 stitches, (dc, ch 2, dc) in next stitch ch 3, skip 1 stitch, (dc, ch 2, dc) in next stitch; repeat from * – (14, 8) times, turn.

ALL SIZES: 35 (37, 41) V-stitches plus 2 edge V-stitches made.

ROW 2: Ch 3 (counts as dc), dc in same stitch, *ch 3, (dc, ch 2, dc) in next ch-2 space; repeat from *, end ch 3, 2 dc in top of turning ch, turn.

ROW 3: Repeat Row 2.

ROW 4: Ch 1, sc in same stitch, *ch 2, [(dtr, ch 5) 3 times, dtr] in next ch-2 space, ch 2, sc in next ch-2 space; repeat from *, end last repeat sc in top of turning ch, turn.

ROW 5: Ch 1, 3 sc in ch-2 sp, *(6 sc in next ch-5 sp) 3 times, (sc in next ch-2 sp) 2 times; repeat from *, ending 3 sc in last ch-2 sp. Fasten off.

FINISHING

Pin back collar seam to center of bound-off Back stitches and Fronts at markers to side edges of Back. Sew edge of Fronts between markers to bound-off edge of Back to form back neck and shoulders, gathering Back as necessary. Sew in sleeves, centering top of cap at back shoulder seam and sleeve seam at center underarm bind-off row and easing in front edge of sleeve as necessary. Weave in ends.

PACIFICA JACKET SCHEMATIC

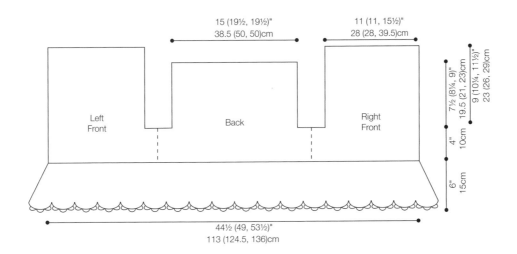

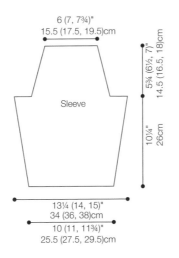

mistral cardigan

page 44

The Mistral Cardigan's curvaceous profile develops in large part from its wide peplum and ribbed waist. The peplum panel is worked back and forth in reverse stockinette stitch for some inches until you cinch the body quickly with k2tog decreases on the wrong side, followed by a ribbed midsection band. Crocheted edging neatens the fronts and collar, and puffy, full-looking pockets are attached, further accenting the hourglass shape. The deep neckline and low armhole situate the bust almost two inches below the usual bustline, which accounts for the small bust dimensions specified in the pattern.

SIZES
XS (S, M, L)

Remember to use this guide to find your size based on your bust measurement: XS = 31"–33" (79cm–84cm); S = 34"–36" (86cm–91cm); M = 37"–39" (94cm–99cm); L = 40"–42" (102cm–107cm).

KNITTED MEASUREMENTS
Bust (buttoned): 23^1/$_4$ (26, 28^1/$_2$, 31)" (59 [66, 72, 78.5]cm)

Back length (not including collar): 20^3/$_4$ (21^1/$_2$, 22^1/$_2$, 23^1/$_4$)" (52.5 [54.5, 57, 59]cm)

MATERIALS
5 (5, 6, 6) hanks Twinkle Handknits Soft Chunky, 100% virgin merino wool, 7 oz/200g, 83 yds/75m, #20 Icy Blue 🔵6

US size 17 (12.75mm) 29" (75cm) circular needle

US size 19 (15mm) 29" (75cm) circular needle or size needed to obtain gauge

Size 7 (4.5mm) crochet hook

Stitch holders

Stitch markers

Tapestry needle

Three 1^5/$_8$" (4cm) buttons

GAUGE
11 stitches and 16^1/$_2$ rows = 7" (18cm) in reverse stockinette stitch (page 150) on size 19 (15mm) needle.

Take the time to check your gauge.

NOTES
The sleeves and body are knit back and forth; a circular needle is used to accommodate the many stitches. The neck shaping is done using short rows.

Twinkle Knit Bit
Great row markers can be made from "no snag" silicone hair bands, which don't cling to yarn. Inexpensive and available in packs of assorted colors, they can be assigned meanings based on their colors—red to mark repeats, for example, and blue to note the beginnings or ends of sections—and they can do double duty, tethering a ponytail or keeping your hair out of your eyes while knitting.

NECK AND RAGLAN SHAPING TABLE

Row #	All Sizes: Work to this many stitches from Right Front Edge, wrap and turn	All Sizes: Work to this many stitches from Left Front Edge, wrap and turn	XS	S	M	L
ROW 5		4	Sleeves	Sleeves	Sleeves	Sleeves
ROW 6	4		Back and Sleeves	Back and Sleeves	Back and Sleeves	Sleeves
ROW 7		5	Sleeves	Sleeves	Sleeves	Back and Sleeves
ROW 8	5		Sleeves	Sleeves	Sleeves	Sleeves
ROW 9		6	Sleeves	Sleeves	Sleeves	Sleeves
ROW 10	6		Back and Sleeves (Back edge only)	Back and Sleeves (Back edge only)	Sleeves (Back edge only)	Sleeves (Back edge only)
ROW 11		8	Sleeves (Back edge only)	Sleeves (Back edge only)	Back and Sleeves (Back edge only)	Sleeves (Back edge only)
ROW 12	8		Sleeves (Back edge only)	Sleeves (Back edge only)	Sleeves (Back edge only)	Sleeves (Back edge only)
ROW 13		10	Sleeves (Back edge only)	Sleeves (Back edge only)	Sleeves (Back edge only)	Back and Sleeves (Back edge only)
ROW 14	10		Back and Sleeves (Back edge only)	Back and Sleeves (Back edge only)	Sleeves (Back edge only)	Sleeves (Back edge only)
ROW 15		12	Sleeves (Back edge only)	Sleeves (Back edge only)	Sleeves (Back edge only)	Sleeves (Back edge only)
ROW 16	12		Sleeves (Back edge only)	Sleeves (Back edge only)	Back and Sleeves (Back edge only)	Sleeves (Back edge only)
ROW 17			Skip to Bands			
ROW 18			--			Back
ROW 19			--	Skip to Bands		
ROW 20			--	--		
ROW 21			--	--	Skip to Bands	
ROW 22			--	--	--	

SLEEVES (MAKE 2)

With smaller needle, and using cable cast-on, cast on 19 (21, 21, 23) stitches.

Work 2 rows in k1, p1 rib (see page 150).

Change to larger needle and reverse stockinette stitch (see page 00).

SIZE XS ONLY: P1, *M1-p, p2; repeat from * to last 2 stitches, (M1-p, p1) twice.
SIZES S AND M ONLY: P1, *M1-p, p2; repeat from * to end.
SIZE L ONLY: P2, *M1-p, p2; repeat from * to last 3 stitches, p3.
ALL SIZES: 29 (31, 31, 33) stitches.

Work even until sleeve measures 8½" (21.5cm) from the beginning.

SHAPE UNDERARM

Bind off 2 stitches at the beginning of the next 2 rows. Place the remaining 25 (27, 27, 29) stitches on holder.

BODY

With smaller needle, and using long-tail cast, cast on 64 (68, 68, 72) stitches.

Knit 3 rows.

Change to larger needle and, beginning with a right-side row, work even in reverse stockinette stitch until piece measures 6¾" (17cm) from the beginning, ending with a right-side row.

NEXT ROW (WS):
SIZE XS ONLY: (K2tog) across.
SIZE S ONLY: K2, *k2tog; repeat from * to last 2 stitches, k2.
SIZE M ONLY: *K1, (k2tog) twice; repeat from * to last 3 stitches, k3tog.
SIZE L ONLY: *K1, (k2tog) twice; repeat

from * to last 2 stitches, k2.
ALL SIZES: 32 (36, 40, 44) stitches.

Work 10 rows in k1, p1 rib (see page 150).

NEXT ROW (RS): P7 (8, 9, 10), place marker to indicate right underarm, p18 (20, 22, 24), place marker for left underarm, p7 (8, 9, 10).

Work even in reverse stockinette stitch for 5 more rows.

NECK SHAPING

NOTE: READ ALL SHAPING INSTRUCTIONS BEFORE BEGINNING.

ROW 1 (RS): Work to 2 stitches from Left Front Edge, wrap and turn (see page Short Rows on page 152).

ROW 2 (WS): Work to 2 stitches from Right Front edge, wrap and turn.

DIVIDE BODY

ROW 3 (RS): Removing markers, *work to 2 stitches before marker, bind off 4 stitches; repeat from *, continue to end of short row, work to 3 stitches from Left Front Edge, wrap and turn.

JOIN SLEEVES AND BODY

ROW 4 (WS): Work to bound-off stitches, place marker to indicate raglan shaping, k25 (27, 27, 29) Left Sleeve stitches, place marker to indicate raglan shaping, k14 (16, 18, 20) Back stitches, place marker to indicate raglan shaping, k25 (27, 27, 29) Right Sleeve stitches, place marker to indicate raglan shaping, work to 3 stitches from Right Front edge, wrap and turn—74 (82, 86, 94) stitches.

Work short-row neck shaping and raglan shaping on Sleeves and Back,

placing decreases as indicated in Neck and Raglan Shaping Table (page 131) and working even where cells are empty.

RS ROWS, IF DECREASE PRECEDES A MARKER: Ssp, p1, slip marker.
RS ROWS, IF DECREASE FOLLOWS A MARKER: Slip marker, p1, p2tog.
WS ROWS, IF DECREASE PRECEDES A MARKER: K2tog, k1, slip marker.
WS ROWS, IF DECREASE FOLLOWS A MARKER: Slip marker, k1, ssk.

ALL SIZES: 34 (42, 46, 54) stitches remain when all shaping is complete.

BANDS

Cut yarn and place stitches on holder.

ROW 1 (RS): With smaller needle, pick up and knit 26 stitches up Right Front edge, place marker; knit neck stitches from holder, increasing 12 (8, 8, 4) stitches evenly spaced—46 (50, 54, 58) stitches total stitches around neck; place marker, pick up and knit 26 stitches down Left Front edge—98 (102, 106, 110) stitches.
ROW 2: P2, *k2, p2; repeat from * across.
ROW 3 (BUTTONHOLE ROW): (K2, p2) twice, *k2tog, yo, p2, k2, p2; repeat from * once, k2tog, yo, continue in rib as established across.
ROWS 4 AND 5: Work in k2, p2 rib as established.
ROW 6: Bind off 25 stitches, remove marker, bind off 1 more stitch, work in rib as established to end—72 (76, 80, 84) stitches.
ROW 7: Bind off 25 stitches, remove marker, bind off 1 more stitch, work in established rib to end—46 (50, 54, 58) stitches.
ROWS 8-16: Work in k2, p2 rib.

SHAPE COLLAR

ROWS 17 AND 18: Work to 2 stitches before end of row, wrap and turn.
ROWS 19 AND 20: Work to 4 stitches before end of row, wrap and turn.
ROWS 21 AND 22: Work to 7 stitches before end of row, wrap and turn.
ROWS 23 AND 24: Work to 10 stitches before end of row, wrap and turn.
ROWS 25 AND 26: Work to 14 stitches before end of row, wrap and turn.

Continue on all stitches, picking up all wraps (see Short Rows on page 152), and work 6 rows even.

Bind off very loosely, using larger needle if necessary.

POCKETS (MAKE 2)

With larger needle, long-tail cast on 7 stitches.

Working in reverse stockinette stitch, cast on 2 stitches at the end of the next 2 rows then 1 stitch at the end of the following 2 rows—13 stitches.

Work even until Pocket measures 5" (12cm) from the beginning, ending with a right-side row.

NEXT ROW: K1, *k2tog, k1; repeat from * 3 times—9 stitches.

Change to smaller needles and work 2 rows in k1, p1 rib (see page 00). Bind off.

FINISHING

With crochet hook and right side facing, single crochet evenly up Right Front edge, around outside of collar, and down Left Front Edge. Fasten off. Sew sleeve and underarm seams. Sew pockets on peplum, with entire pocket in front of center underarm and the bottom of the pocket just above the garter edge, easing in the shaped lower edge to form a rounded pouch. Weave in ends. Sew on buttons, creating shanks if necessary to accommodate the thickness of the knit fabric.

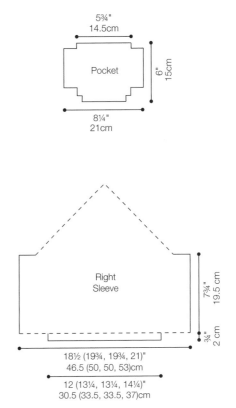

MISTRAL CARDIGAN SCHEMATIC

sirocco cardigan

page 44

A close relative of the Mistral (page 44, 30), the Sirocco Cardigan also features a wasp-waisted profile owing to its peplum and snug waist accented by a button closure. Its voluminous sleeves contrast with the abbreviated length, making it a strikingly sophisticated outer layer to a close-fitted top and narrow pant combo. Fastened low, this cardi lengthens the torso for a flattering look. The bustline is also situated low—a couple of inches below where it's usually measured—resulting from the low armhole's connection to the body of the sweater. That construction detail, along with the fact that the Sirocco, like the Mistral, relies on a snug fit to sculpt the bodice, explains the negative ease through the bust.

SIZES
XS (S, M, L)

Remember to use this guide to find your size based on your bust measurement: XS = 31"–33" (79cm–84cm); S = 34"–36" (86cm–91cm); M = 37"–39" (94cm–99cm); L = 40"–42" (102cm–107cm).

KNITTED MEASUREMENTS
Bust (buttoned): 23¼ (26, 28½, 31)" (59 [66, 72, 78.5]cm)
Back length: 20 (20, 20½, 21)" (50.5 [50.5, 52, 52]cm)

MATERIALS
4 (4, 4, 5) hanks Twinkle Handknits Soft Chunky, 100% virgin merino wool, 7 oz/200g, 83 yds/75m, #08 White ⑥

US size 17 (12.75mm) 29" (75cm) circular needle

US size 19 (15mm) 29" (75cm) circular needle or size needed to obtain gauge

Stitch holders

Stitch markers

Tapestry needle

Two 1⅝" (4cm) buttons

GAUGE
11 stitches and 16½ rows = 7" (18cm) in reverse stockinette stitch on size 19 (15mm) needle.

Take the time to check your gauge.

NOTES
A circular needle is used to accommodate the many stitches. The neck shaping is done using short rows. Side-opening pockets are knit at same time as the front pieces.

Twinkle Knit Bit
Does tackling blocking seem like a team sport? Some pros use everyday items to help. For example, carpet remnants or samples having bound edges, turned to the wrong side, make great surfaces for blocking knits. Stainless steel pins easily penetrate the backing to hold knits fast. To stretch or shape hats, try an aluminum (make certain the metal is rustproof) pizza pan or the base of a springform pan, both of which come in a variety of sizes. Likewise, the plastic gridded baffles used to diffuse light from overhead fluorescent fixtures can serve as drying racks.

SLEEVES (MAKE 2)

With smaller needle, and using cable cast-on, cast on 19 (21, 21, 23) stitches.

Work 2 rows in k1, p1 rib (see page 150).

Change to larger needles and reverse stockinette stitch (see page 150).

SIZE XS ONLY: P1, *M1-p, p2; repeat from * to last 2 stitches, (M1-p, p1) twice.
SIZES S AND M ONLY: P1, *M1-p, p2; repeat from * to end.
SIZE L ONLY: P2, *M1-p, p2; repeat from * to last 3 stitches, p3.
ALL SIZES: 29 (31, 31, 33) stitches.

Work even until sleeve measures 8½" (21.5cm) from the beginning.

SHAPE UNDERARM

Bind off 2 stitches at the beginning of the next 2 rows.

Place remaining 25 (27, 27, 29) stitches on holder.

BODY

With larger needle, and using long-tail cast-on, cast on 64 (68, 72, 76) stitches.

Beginning with a wrong-side row, work 3 rows in stockinette stitch.

Knit 4 rows.

MAKE POCKETS
RIGHT FRONT POCKET

ROW 1 (RS): P6, turn, leaving remaining stitches unworked.
ROWS 2 AND 4: K6.
ROWS 3 AND 5: P6.
ROW 6: K6. Slip these 6 stitches to holder. Cut yarn.

Turn and slip all stitches to the other end of the needle.

LEFT FRONT POCKET

ROW 1 (WS): K6, turn, leaving remaining stitches unworked.
ROWS 2 AND 4: P6.
ROWS 3 AND 5: K6.
ROW 6: P6. Slip these 6 stitches to holder. Cut yarn.
Turn and slip all stitches to the other end of the needle.
With right side facing and holding pocket stitches to front and working into purl bumps at base of pocket, pick up and purl 6 stitches from behind Right Front pocket, p52 (56, 60, 64) stitches, pick up and purl 6 stitches from behind Left Front pocket—64 (68, 72, 76) stitches.
Work 5 rows even in reverse stockinette stitch.
NEXT ROW (RS): Holding Right Front pocket stitches parallel to and in front of body stitches, (purl together 1 stitch from holder and 1 stitch from needle) 6 times, purl to last 6 stitches, purl pocket stitches and body stitches together as for Right Front.

Knit 1 row.

BODY RIB
NEXT ROW (RS):
SIZE XS ONLY: (K2tog) across.
SIZE S ONLY: K2, *k2tog; repeat from * to last 2 stitches, k2.
SIZE M ONLY: K3, *(k2tog) 16 times, k1; repeat from * once, k3.
SIZE L ONLY: K2, *k1, (k2tog) four times; repeat from * 7 times, k2.
ALL SIZES: 32 (36, 40, 44) stitches.

Work 9 rows in k1, p1 rib (see page 00).

NEXT ROW (RS): P7 (8, 9, 10), place marker to indicate right underarm, p18 (20, 22, 24), place marker to indicate left underarm, purl to end.

Work even in reverse stockinette stitch for 3 rows.

NECK AND ARMHOLE SHAPING

NOTE: READ ALL SHAPING INSTRUCTIONS BEFORE BEGINNING.

NEXT 2 ROWS: Work to 2 stitches from Left Front edge, wrap and turn (see Short Rows on page 152); work to 2 stitches from Right Front edge, wrap and turn.
NEXT 2 ROWS: Work to 3 stitches from Left Front edge, wrap and turn; work to 3 stitches from Right Front edge, wrap and turn.

DIVIDE BODY

ROW 1 (RS): Removing markers, *purl to 2 stitches before marker, bind off 4 stitches; repeat from * once, purl to 4 stitches from Left Front edge, wrap and turn.

JOIN SLEEVES AND BODY

ROW 2: Work to bound-off stitches, place marker to indicate raglan shaping, k25 (27, 27, 29) Left Sleeve stitches, place marker to indicate raglan shaping, k14 (16, 18, 20) Back stitches, place marker to indicate raglan shaping, k25 (27, 27, 29) Right Sleeve stitches, place marker to indicate raglan shaping, knit to 4 stitches from Right Front edge, wrap and turn—74 (82, 86, 94) stitches.

Work short-row neck shaping and raglan shaping on Sleeves and Back, placing decreases as indicated in Neck and Raglan Shaping Table (page 136) and working even where cells are empty.

RS ROWS, IF DECREASE PRECEDES A MARKER:
Ssp, p1, slip marker.
RS ROWS, IF DECREASE FOLLOWS A MARKER:
Slip marker, p1, p2tog.

NECK AND RAGLAN SHAPING TABLE

Row #	All Sizes: Work to this many stitches from Right Front Edge, wrap and turn	All Sizes: Work to this many stitches from Left Front Edge, wrap and turn	XS	S	M	L
ROW 3		5	Sleeves	Sleeves	Sleeves	Sleeves
ROW 4	5		Back and Sleeves	Back and Sleeves	Back and Sleeves	Back and Sleeves
ROW 5		6	Sleeves	Sleeves	Sleeves	Sleeves
ROW 6	6		Sleeves	Sleeves	Sleeves	Sleeves
ROW 7		7	Sleeves (Back edge only)	Sleeves	Sleeves	Sleeves
ROW 8	7		Back and Sleeves (Back edge only)	Sleeves (Back edge only)	Back and Sleeves (Back edge only)	Back and Sleeves (Back edge only)
ROW 9		9	Sleeves (Back edge only)	Back and Sleeves (Back edge only)	Sleeves (Back edge only)	Sleeves (Back edge only)
ROW 10	9		Sleeves (Back edge only)	Sleeves (Back edge only)	Sleeves (Back edge only)	Sleeves (Back edge only)
ROW 11		11	Sleeves (Back edge only)	Sleeves (Back edge only)	Sleeves (Back edge only)	Sleeves (Back edge only)
ROW 12	11		Back and Sleeves (Back edge only)	Sleeves (Back edge only)	Sleeves (Back edge only)	Back and Sleeves (Back edge only)
ROW 13		13	Sleeves (Back edge only)	Sleeves (Back edge only)	Sleeves (Back edge only)	Sleeves (Back edge only)
ROW 14	13			Back	Back	
ROW 15		15				
ROW 16	15					Back
ROW 17			Skip to Bands	Skip to Bands		
ROW 18					Skip to Bands	

WS ROWS, IF DECREASE PRECEDES A MARKER:
K2tog, k1, slip marker.
WS ROWS, IF DECREASE FOLLOWS A MARKER:
Slip marker, k1, ssk.

ALL SIZES: 38 (44, 48, 54) stitches remain when all shaping is complete.

BANDS

Cut yarn and leave stitches on needle.

ROW 1 (RS): With smaller needle, pick up and knit 26 stitches up Right Front edge; working stitches from larger needle and picking up all wraps (see page 152), k2 (2, 3, 3), M1, k2, M1, knit to last 4 (4, 5, 5) stitches on holder, M1, k2, M1, k2 (2, 3, 3); pick up and knit 25 stitches down Left Front edge—93 (99, 103, 109) stitches.
ROW 2: P1, ★k1, p1; repeat from ★ across.
ROW 3 (BUTTONHOLE ROW): (K1, p1) 4 times, ★k2tog, yo, (k1, p1) 3 times; repeat from ★ once, continue in rib as established across.

ROWS 4, 5, AND 6: Work in rib as established.

Bind off.

FINISHING
Sew front-band edges of pockets to wrong side.

With right side facing and using smaller needle, pick up and knit 7 stitches along open edge of one pocket. Work 1 row in k1, p1 rib (see page 150). Bind off.

Sew edges of pocket ribbing to body of sweater.

Repeat for second pocket.

Sew sleeve and underarm seams. Weave in ends. Sew on buttons, creating shanks if necessary to accommodate the thickness of the knit fabric.

SIROCCO CARDIGAN SCHEMATIC

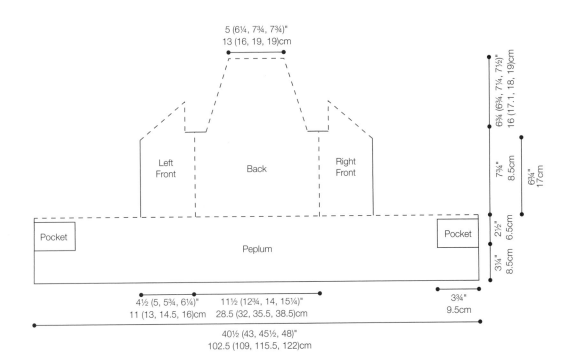

stockholm sweater

page 46

The Stockholm is worked with four strands of Twinkle Cruise yarn held as one. The Stockholm Sweater's upper body features a handsome ribbed neckline edge and cabled section that both provides some sturdiness and frames the keyhole opening before the lightening bolt lacework pattern begins. This pattern was designed to situate the cables evenly on the front regardless of size, so don't be concerned that each size places decreases for the gently scooped neck on different rows. A separate cabled band, a final grace note, is then made and sewn to the sweater's lower edge. This sweater's relaxed fit allows for a thin layer to be worn underneath, for modesty or to add an accent color.

SIZES

XS (S, M, L)

Remember to use this guide to find your size based on your bust measurement: XS = 31"–33" (79cm–84cm); S = 34"–36" (86cm–91cm); M = 37"–39" (94cm–99cm); L = 40"–42" (102cm–107cm).

KNITTED MEASUREMENTS

Bust: 35$\frac{1}{4}$ (38$\frac{1}{2}$, 41$\frac{1}{2}$, 44$\frac{3}{4}$)" (89.5 [97.5, 105, 113.5]cm)

Back length: 19$\frac{1}{4}$ (19$\frac{1}{4}$, 19$\frac{3}{4}$, 20$\frac{1}{4}$)" (48.5 [48.5, 50, 51]cm)

MATERIALS

12 (13, 15, 16) balls Twinkle Handknits Cruise, 70% silk/30% cotton, 1$\frac{3}{4}$ oz/50g, 120 yds/109m, #44 Stone Grey ⑥

US size 15 (10mm) 29" (75cm) circular needle or size needed to obtain gauge

Stitch holders

Stitch markers

Tapestry needle

One 1" (2.5cm) button

GAUGE

10 stitches and 13$\frac{3}{4}$ rows = 4" (10cm) over Chart A on size 15 (10mm) needle with 4 strands held together.

ABBREVIATION

Dec 1 (decrease 1): P2tog on right side, k2tog on wrong side.

NOTES

The entire piece is worked with four strands of yarn held together. First, the sleeves are worked back and forth on a circular needle; then the body is worked in the round. The sleeves are joined to the body at the underarm and the sweater is knit in one piece from that point. Mark the beginning of the round with a stitch marker in a color different from the others.

SLEEVES (MAKE 2)

With 4 strands held together, and using cable cast-on, cast on 28 (32, 36, 40) stitches.

Work 7 rows in stockinette stitch (see page 150), then 4 rows in k1, p1 rib (see page 150).

Beginning with a wrong-side row, begin Chart A.

Work even until Sleeve measures 12¾" (32cm) from the beginning, ending with a wrong-side row.

UNDERARM SHAPING

Bind off 2 stitches at the beginning of the next 2 rows. Place the remaining 24 (28, 32, 36) stitches on holder.

BODY

With 4 strands held together, cable cast on 22 (24, 26, 28) right Front stitches, place marker to indicate right underarm, cast on 44 (48, 52, 56) Back stitches, place marker to indicate left underarm, cast on 22 (24, 26, 28) left Front stitches, place marker to indicate center front and beginning of round—88 (96, 104, 112) stitches. Join, being careful not to twist stitches.

Beginning with Rnd 1, work Chart A until Body measures approximately 11" (28cm) from beginning, ending with an even-numbered round.

DIVIDE BODY

Removing the underarm markers as you go, *purl to 2 stitches before underarm marker, bind off 4 stitches; repeat from *, purl to end of round— 40 (44, 48, 52) stitches each for Front and Back.

JOIN SLEEVES AND BODY

P20 (22, 24, 26) right Front stitches, p24 (28, 32, 36) Right Sleeve stitches, p40 (44, 48, 52) Back stitches, p24 (28,

32, 36) Left Sleeve stitches, purl to 4 stitches before end of round—128 (144, 160, 176) stitches total.

BEGIN PLACKET AND ESTABLISH PATTERNS

ROW 1 (RS): Bind off 8 stitches for Placket, p2 (3, 2, 2) including the last stitch on the needle following bind off, *work Row 1 of Chart B across next 4 stitches, p4 (5, 5, 6); repeat from * to last 6 (7, 6, 6) stitches, work Row 1 of Chart B across next 4 stitches, p2 (3, 2, 2), turn—120 (136, 152, 168) stitches.

YOKE AND NECK SHAPING

NOTE: READ ALL SHAPING INSTRUCTIONS BEFORE BEGINNING.

ROW 2: Work even in patterns as established, keeping first and last 2 (3, 2, 2) stitches of row in reverse stockinette stitch.

Decrease in EVERY reverse stockinette section between cables on rows indicated in the Yoke and Neck Shaping Table (page 140), and work even on rows where cells are empty.

AT THE SAME TIME on row marked ★★, dec 1 at each neck edge once.

ALL SIZES: 76 (78, 86, 86) stitches remain when all shaping is complete. Place remaining stitches on holder.

PLACKET EDGES

With right side facing and 4 strands held together, pick up and knit 13 (13, 14, 15) stitches along left placket edge. Work 3 rows in k1, p1 rib (see page 150). Bind off.

Repeat for right placket, keeping last stitch on needle; do not cut yarn.

NECKBAND AND BUTTONHOLE TAB

With right side facing and 4 strands held together, cable cast on 5 stitches.

ROW 1 (RS): (K1, p1) 3 times, pick up and knit 3 stitches along top of placket, work in k1, p1 rib across stitches on holder, making decreases as described below, pick up and knit 3 stitches along top of placket.

SIZE M ONLY: At the same time, when working stitches from holder, dec16 times, maintaining ribbing and placing decreases between the 1st and 2nd cables, between the 4th and 5th cables, between the 7th and 8th cables, between the 10th and 11th cables, between the 13th and 14th cables, and between the 16th and 17th cables.
SIZE L ONLY: At the same time, when working stitches from holder, decrease 14 times, maintaining ribbing and placing decreases between the 1st and 2nd cables, between the 6th and 7th cables, between the 11th and 12th cables, and between the 16th and 17th cables.
ALL SIZES: 88 (90, 92, 94) stitches.
ROW 2: Work in rib as established.
ROW 3 (BUTTONHOLE ROW): K1, p1, yo, p2tog, work in rib as established to end.
ROW 4: Work in rib as established. Bind off.

LOWER BAND

With 4 strands held together, cable cast on 8 stitches.

Work Chart C 19 (20, 21, 22) times. Bind off.

FINISHING

Sew sleeve and underarm seams. Sew lower placket edges to bound-off edge. Sew ends of band together, then sew band sideways along lower edge of body. Sew button on left side of neckband opposite buttonhole. Weave in ends.

YOKE AND NECK SHAPING TABLE

	XS	S	M	L
ROW 3	Dec 1	Dec 1	Dec 1	Dec 1
ROW 4				
ROW 5				Dec 1
ROW 6				
ROW 7	Dec 1	Dec 1	Dec 1	
ROW 8**				
ROW 9				Dec 1
ROW 10				
ROW 11	Dec 1	Dec 1	Dec 1	
ROW 12				
ROW 13		Dec 1		Dec 1
ROW 14				
ROW 15	Skip to Neckband	Skip to Neckband	Dec 1	
ROW 16	--	--		
ROW 17	--	--	Skip to Neckband	Dec 1
ROW 18	--	--	--	

STOCKHOLM SWEATER
STITCH PATTERN

STOCKHOLM SWEATER
SCHEMATIC

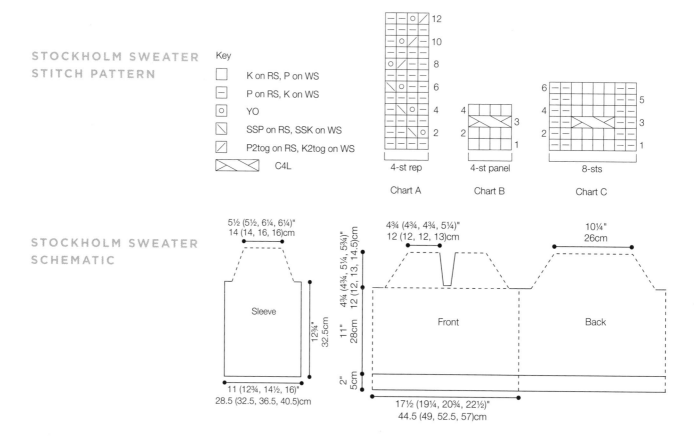

Key

☐ K on RS, P on WS

⊟ P on RS, K on WS

○ YO

◹ SSP on RS, SSK on WS

◿ P2tog on RS, K2tog on WS

⬭ C4L

4-st rep

Chart A

4-st panel

Chart B

8-sts

Chart C

5½ (5½, 6¼, 6¼)"
14 (14, 16, 16)cm

Sleeve

12¾"
32.5cm

11 (12¾, 14½, 16)"
28.5 (32.5, 36.5, 40.5)cm

4¾ (4¾, 4¾, 5¼)"
12 (12, 12, 13)cm

4¾ (4¾, 5¼, 5¾)"
12 (12, 13, 14.5)cm

11"
28cm

2"
5cm

Front

10¼"
26cm

Back

17½ (19¼, 20¾, 22½)"
44.5 (49, 52.5, 57)cm

san tropez pullover

page 47

This vibrant knit showcases the bulky yarn's unexpected stretch and softness. The pattern's slender dimensions and ribbed cuffs and deep hem hold the knit neatly against the body; you can comfortably wear the San Tropez over a thin, nude-colored camisole or a colored T-shirt with the color peeking through the sexy chevron openwork. When knitting the fitted shoulder and neck region, you'll work some short rows to refine the fit. Whenever you come across such instructions in a Twinkle pattern, be sure to count those short rows as if they were full ones when determining in which row to make raglan decreases. Short rows also are worked into the neck placket, widening it into a cute collar to wear up or down.

SIZES

XS (S, M, L)

Remember to use this guide to find your size based on your bust measurement: XS = 31"–33" (79cm–84cm); S = 34"–36" (86cm–91cm); M = 37"–39" (94cm–99cm); L = 40"–42" (102cm–107cm).

KNITTED MEASUREMENTS

Bust: 27$\frac{1}{2}$ (30$\frac{1}{2}$, 33, 35$\frac{1}{2}$)" (69.5 [77, 83.5, 90]cm)

Back length (not including collar): 23$\frac{1}{2}$ (24$\frac{1}{4}$, 25, 25$\frac{3}{4}$)" (59.5 [61, 63, 65]cm)

MATERIALS

3 (3, 4, 4) hanks Twinkle Handknits Soft Chunky, 100% virgin merino wool, 7 oz/200g, 83 yds/75m, #07 Canary ⑥

US size 17 (12.75mm) 24" (60cm)circular needle

US size 19 (15mm) 24" (60cm) circular needle or size needed to obtain gauge

Stitch holders

Stitch markers

Tapestry needle

One 1$\frac{1}{2}$" (4cm) button

GAUGE

11 stitches and 16$\frac{1}{2}$ rows = 7" (18cm) in stockinette stitch on size 19 (15mm) needle.

Take the time to check your gauge.

ABBREVIATIONS

Inc 1 (increase 1): Maintaining pattern, knit (or purl) 1 into right loop of stitch in row below next stitch on left-hand needle, then knit (or purl) the next stitch on left-hand needle.

RS Dec Row: *Knit to 3 stitches before marker, k2tog, k1, slip marker, k1, ssk; repeat from * 3 times, knit to end.

WS Dec Row: *Purl to 3 stitches before marker, ssp, p1, slip marker, p1, p2tog; repeat from * 3 times, purl to end.

Chevron Pattern (9-stitch panel; see chart, page 144)

RND 1: K4, yo, ssk, k3.

RND 2 and all even-numbered rnds: Knit.

RND 3: K2, k2tog, yo, k1, yo, ssk, k2.

RND 5: K1, k2tog, yo, k3, yo, ssk, k1.

RND 7: K2tog, yo, k5, yo, ssk.

RND 8: Knit.

Repeat Rnds 1–8 for pattern.

First, the sleeves are worked back and forth on a circular needle; then, the body is worked in the round to the underarms. The sleeves are joined to the body at the underarm and the sweater is worked back and forth in one piece from that point; change to a shorter circular needle when it is comfortable to do so. The front neck drop is formed by short rows; these short rows are counted like full rows when you are determining where to make decreases for raglan shaping. Mark the beginning of the round with a stitch marker in a color different from the others.

SLEEVES (MAKE 2)

With smaller needle, and using cable cast-on), cast on 13 (15, 17, 19) stitches.

ROW 1 (RS): K1, *p1, k1; repeat from * across.

Work 11 more rows in k1, p1 rib as established.

Change to larger needle and work 12 rows even in stockinette stitch, ending with a wrong-side row.

NEXT ROW (INC ROW): K1, inc 1, knit to last stitch, increase 1, k1—15 (17, 19, 21) stitches.

Work 7 rows even, then repeat Increase Row Row once more—17 (19, 21, 23) stitches.

Work even until Sleeve measures 16½" (42cm) from the beginning, ending with a wrong-side row.

UNDERARM SHAPING

Bind off 2 stitches at the beginning of the next row and 1 stitch at the beginning of the following row.

Place the remaining 14 (16, 18, 20) stitches on holder.

BODY

With smaller needle, cable cast on 11 (12, 13, 14) Front stitches, place marker to indicate center front, cable cast on 11 (12, 13, 14) Front stitches, place marker to indicate right underarm, cable cast on 22 (24, 26, 28) Back stitches, place marker to indicate left underarm and beginning of round—44 (48, 52, 56) stitches. Join, being careful not to twist stitches.

Work 15 rounds in k1, p1 rib.

Change to larger needle and stockinette stitch.

NEXT RND (ESTABLISH PATTERN): Knit to 10 sts before center front marker, work Rnd 1 of Chevron Pattern across next 9 stitches, k1, slip marker, k1, work Rnd 1 of Chevron Pattern across next 9 stitches, knit to end of round.

Continue in established patterns until 3 full repeats of Chevron Pattern are complete, ending last round 1 stitch before end of round.

DIVIDE BODY

ROW 1 (RS): Removing markers, bind off 2 stitches for left underarm, work to 2 stitches before center front marker, bind off 4 stitches for placket opening, work to 1 stitch before next marker, bind off 2 stitches, work to end of round. Cut yarn, turn.

JOIN SLEEVES AND BODY

ROW 2 (WS): Join yarn at Left Front placket opening, p8 (9, 10, 11) Left Front stitches, place marker to indicate raglan shaping, p14 (16, 18, 20) Left Sleeve stitches, place marker to indicate raglan shaping, p20 (22, 24, 26) Back stitches, place marker to indicate raglan

shaping, p14 (16, 18, 20) Right Sleeve stitches, place marker to indicate raglan shaping, purl to end of row—64 (72, 80, 88) stitches.

NECK AND RAGLAN SHAPING

NOTE: READ ALL SHAPING INSTRUCTIONS BEFORE BEGINNING.

Work raglan shaping on Fronts, Back and Sleeves, working decreases as indicated in the Neck and Raglan Shaping Table (page 143) and working even on row where cells are empty.

RS ROWS, IF DECREASE PRECEDES A MARKER:
K2tog, k1, slip marker.
RS ROWS, IF DECREASE FOLLOWS A MARKER:
Slip marker, k1, ssk.
WS ROWS, IF DECREASE PRECEDES A MARKER:
Ssp, p1, slip marker.
WS ROWS, IF DECREASE FOLLOWS A MARKER:
Slip marker, p1, p2tog.

AT THE SAME TIME, on row marked **, work short rows as follows, maintaining raglan shaping:

Work to 3 stitches from Left Front edge, wrap and turn (see Short Rows on page 152); work to 3 stitches from Right Front edge, wrap and turn; work to 5 stitches from Left Front edge, wrap and turn; work to 5 stitches from Right Front edge, wrap and turn. Continue on all stitches, picking up all wraps (see page 152).

ALL SIZES: 30 (32, 32, 34) stitches remain when all shaping is complete.

Cut yarn and leave stitches on needle.

FINISHING
PLACKET BANDS AND SHAWL COLLAR

With right side facing and using smaller needle, pick up and knit 12

NECK AND RAGLAN SHAPING TABLE

	XS	S	M	L
ROW 3	Front, Back, and Sleeves	Front, Back, and Sleeves	Front, Back, and Sleeves	Front, Back, and Sleeves
ROW 4				
ROW 5				
ROW 6	Front, Back, and Sleeves	Front, Back, and Sleeves	Front, Back, and Sleeves	Front, Back, and Sleeves
ROW 7				
ROW 8				
ROW 9	Front, Back, and Sleeves	Front, Back, and Sleeves	Front, Back, and Sleeves	Front, Back, and Sleeves
ROW 10				
ROW 11**				
ROW 12	Front, Back, and Sleeves	Front, Back, and Sleeves	Front, Back, and Sleeves	Front, Back, and Sleeves
ROW 13				
ROW 14				
ROW 15	Back	Front, Back, and Sleeves	Front, Back, and Sleeves	Front, Back, and Sleeves
ROW 16				
ROW 17	Skip to Placket Bands and Shawl Collar			Front and Sleeves
ROW 18	--		Front, Back, and Sleeves	Back
ROW 19	--	Skip to Placket Bands and Shawl Collar		
ROW 20	--	--		Front and Sleeves
ROW 21	--	--	Skip to Placket Bands and Shawl Collar	
ROW 22	--	--	--	

(12, 16, 16) stitches along right placket edge, place marker for short-row shaping, k30 (32, 32, 34) stitches from needle, place marker for short-row shaping, pick up and knit 12 (12, 16, 16) stitches along left placket edge—54 (56, 64, 66) stitches.

ROW 1 (WS): ★P1, k1; repeat from ★ to end.
ROW 2 (BUTTONHOLE ROW): P1, (k1, p1) twice, yo, p2tog, continue in rib to end.
ROW 3: Work to 1 stitch before second marker, wrap and turn
ROW 4: Work to 1 stitch before marker, wrap and turn.
ROWS 5 AND 6: Work to 3 stitches before marker, wrap and turn.
ROWS 7 AND 8: Work to 5 stitches before marker, wrap and turn.
ROWS 9 AND 10: Work to 7 stitches before marker, wrap and turn.
ROWS 11: Work to end of row, picking up wraps as you come to them.

Bind off very loosely knitwise, picking up remaining wraps.

Sew sleeve and underarm seams. Overlap left placket band with right placket band and sew both to placket bind off. Weave in ends. Sew button opposite buttonhole, creating a shank if necessary to accommodate the thickness of the knit fabric.

CHEVRON STITCH PATTERN

Key

☐ K on RS, P on WS
⊙ YO
◹ SSK
◸ K2tog

9-st panel

Twinkle Knit Bit

Once you've settled down for some knitting, the last thing you want to do is chase errant balls of yarn rolling under the settee. Keep your yarn clean and close at hand by making center-pull balls. Use a large prescription-drug bottle as a form to wind your skein around. First, insert into the bottle a few inches of yarn from an end, cap it, and then begin winding loosely. Vary the angle as you wind to maintain an evenly formed ball, making sure to keep the capped end accessible. Tuck the loose outside end under several rounds of wound yarn and remove the bottle, carefully pulling out the working end. To keep your ball from wandering, confine it in a clean plastic food storage container. Some knitters use a large disposable container with an exit hole for the working end of the yarn pierced into the lid. (Choose a container larger than the 32 oz/946ml variety to be certain that a ball of bulky yarn will fit.) Others prefer to cut out an opening in the side of a two-liter bottle to insert the yarn ball, threading the working end of the yarn out through the top. Placing a clean stone or another smooth, weighty item in the bottom of the container will help to anchor your yarn caddy.

SAN TROPEZ PULLOVER SCHEMATIC

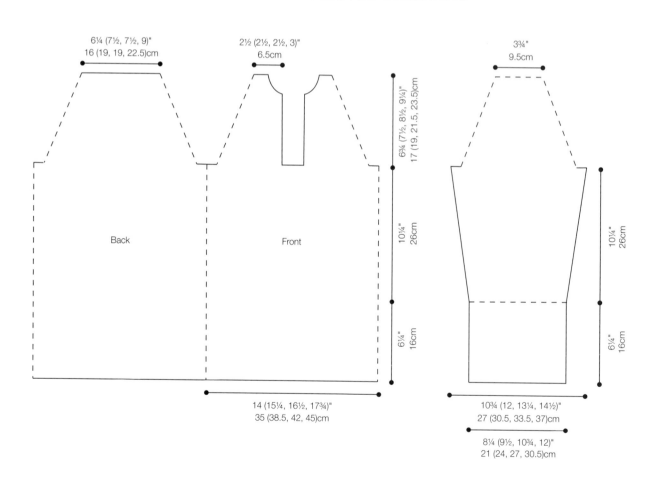

6¼ (7½, 7½, 9)"
16 (19, 19, 22.5)cm

2½ (2½, 2½, 3)"
6.5cm

3¾"
9.5cm

6¾ (7½, 8½, 9¼)"
17 (19, 21.5, 23.5)cm

10¼"
26cm

6¼"
16cm

Back

Front

14 (15¼, 16½, 17¾)"
35 (38.5, 42, 45)cm

10¾ (12, 13¼, 14½)"
27 (30.5, 33.5, 37)cm

8¼ (9½, 10¾, 12)"
21 (24, 27, 30.5)cm

10¼"
26cm

6¼"
16cm

voyageur dress

page 47

The Voyageur's dramatic cables aren't hard to work, but they're hard to miss, twisting on a reverse stockinette stitch ground from the hem to the funnel neck. Another drama unfolds on the reverse, where the ribbed armhole edge crosses from one side of the back to the other, creating a seductive backless section. An ample funnel neck collapses luxuriously at the top of this dress, which is worked on circular needles and in the round up to the underarms. Crocheted straps complete this alluring look.

SIZES

XS (S, M, L)

Remember to use this guide to find your size based on your bust measurement: XS = 31"–33" (79cm–84cm); S = 34"–36" (86cm–91cm); M = 37"–39" (94cm–99cm); L = 40"–42" (102cm–107cm).

KNITTED MEASUREMENTS

Bust: 28 (30$\frac{1}{2}$, 33, 35$\frac{1}{2}$)" (71 [77, 83.5, 90]cm)

Length to collar: 30$\frac{1}{4}$ (30$\frac{3}{4}$, 31$\frac{1}{4}$, 31$\frac{3}{4}$)" (76.5 [78, 79, 79]cm)

MATERIALS

4 (4, 5, 5) hanks Twinkle Handknits Soft Chunky, 100% virgin merino wool, 7 oz/200g, 83 yds/75m, #03 Crimson 6️⃣

US size 17 (12.75mm) 29" (75cm) circular needle

US size 19 (15mm) 29" (75cm) circular needles or size needed to obtain gauge

Size 7 (4.5mm) crochet hook

Cable needle

Stitch holders

Stitch markers

Tapestry needle

GAUGE

11 stitches and 16$\frac{1}{2}$ rows = 7" (18cm) in reverse stockinette stitch on size 19 (15mm) needle.

Take the time to check your gauge.

ABBREVIATIONS

RS Dec Row: P1, p2tog, work to last 3 stitches, ssp, p1.
WS Dec Row: K1, ssk, work to last 3 stitches, k2tog, k1.
C4L (cable 4 left): Slip next 2 stitches to cable needle and hold in front of work, k2, k2 from cable needle.
T3R (twist 3 right): Slip next stitch onto cable needle and hold in back, k2, p1 from cable needle.
T3L (twist 3 left): Slip next 2 stitches onto cable needle and hold in front, p1, k2 from cable needle.
Cable Pattern
(12-stitch panel; see chart, page 147)

NOTES

The dress is knit in the round to underarm, then the Front Bodice is worked back and forth on a circular needle. The front neck shaping is done with short rows. One stitch marker should be a color different from the others to indicate the beginning of the round.

BODY

With smaller needle, and using cable cast-on method, cast on 32 (34, 36, 38) Front stitches, place marker to indicate right underarm, cast on 32 (34, 36, 38) Back stitches, place marker to indicate left underarm and beginning of round—64 (68, 72, 76) stitches. Join, being careful not to twist stitches.

Work 4 rounds in k1, p1 rib (page 150).

Change to larger needle and reverse stockinette stitch (page 150).

NEXT RND (ESTABLISH PATTERN): P10 (11, 12, 13), work Rnd 1 of chart across next 12 stitches, purl to end of round.
Work 15 rounds even in established pattern.
DEC RND: *P1, ssp, purl to 3 stitches before next marker, p2tog, p1, slip marker; repeat from * once—60 (64, 68, 72) stitches.

Repeat Dec Rnd every 7 rounds 4 times more—44 (48, 52, 56) stitches.

Work even until piece measures 22¾" (51.5cm) from beginning.

DIVIDE BODY

NEXT RND: Work in pattern to end of round, remove marker, p2; place last 26 (28, 30, 32) stitches worked onto holder, removing marker from right underarm—18 (20, 22, 24) Front stitches.

FRONT BODICE

NOTE: FRONT IS WORKED BACK AND FORTH IN ROWS FROM THIS POINT. READ ALL SHAPING INSTRUCTIONS BEFORE BEGINNING.

Work 7 (7, 5, 7) rows even, then work WS Dec Row—16 (18, 20, 22) stitches.

Work 6 (6, 5, 5) rows even, then work RS Dec Row or WS Dec Row.

SIZES M AND L ONLY: Work 3 rows even, then work WS Decrease Row.

ALL SIZES: AT THE SAME TIME, when 14 (14, 16, 17) rows of the Front Bodice are complete, work short rows as follows, maintaining side edge shaping:

*Work to 2 stitches from center front edge, wrap and turn (see Short Rows on page 152); repeat from * once.

Continue on all stitches, picking up all wraps (see page 153).

ALL SIZES: 14 (16, 16, 18) stitches remain when shaping is complete.

Work 1 (2, 1, 0) row(s) even. Place stitches on holder.

RIBBING

With right side facing and using smaller needle and a separate ball of yarn, pick up and knit 13 (14, 15, 16) stitches along right Front Bodice edge, knit 26 (28, 30, 32) stitches from holder, pick up and knit 14 (15, 16, 17) stitches along left Front Bodice edge—53 (57, 61, 65) stitches.

Work 4 rows k1, p1 rib (see page 150).

Bind off.

COLLAR

NOTE: COLLAR IS WORKED IN THE ROUND.

With right side facing and using larger needle, pick up and knit 3 stitches along top of left Front Bodice ribbing, k14 (16, 16, 18) Front Bodice stitches from holder, pick up and knit 3 stitches along top of right Front Bodice

ribbing, cast on 20 stitches, place marker for beginning of round and join, being careful not to twist stitches—40 (42, 42, 44) stitches.

Work 31 rounds stockinette stitch.

Bind off very loosely.

FINISHING
BACK STRAPS

With crochet hook, crochet two chains each 8" (20.5cm) long. Sew one end to the 3rd stitch from each corner of neck. Sew other ends to Back ribbing, centering 11 (13,15, 17) stitches between straps. Adjust length as necessary for proper fit.

Weave in ends.

Twinkle Knit Bit
Documenting the knits you've completed not only helps you remember the patterns you worked and their results but also lets you share what you've achieved. Take pictures of finished garments laid flat and photographed from above; shooting from the vantage point of a step-stool down to a knit spread on a clean towel on the floor or ground is one way to accomplish this. In addition, take a snap where the knit is worn, ideally on its recipient. Photographing in even, outdoor light most accurately captures colors, so look for an outside location or one near a window.

Key

☐   K on RS, P on WS

⊟   P on RS, K on WS

T3R

T3L

C4L

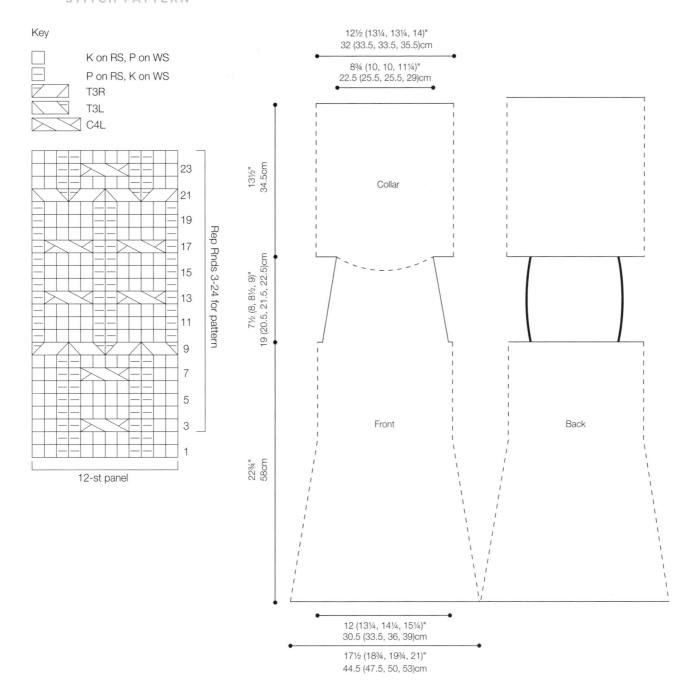

Rep Rnds 3-24 for pattern

23
21
19
17
15
13
11
9
7
5
3
1

12-st panel

12½ (13¼, 13¼, 14)"
32 (33.5, 33.5, 35.5)cm

8¾ (10, 10, 11¼)"
22.5 (25.5, 25.5, 29)cm

13½"
34.5cm

Collar

7½ (8, 8½, 9)"
19 (20.5, 21.5, 22.5)cm

22¾"
58cm

Front

Back

12 (13¼, 14¼, 15¼)"
30.5 (33.5, 36, 39)cm

17½ (18¾, 19¾, 21)"
44.5 (47.5, 50, 53)cm

twinkle
tips and
techniques

PREPARING FOR A PROJECT

First, take the time to build up your confidence and basic skills. Start every design by reviewing its schematic, chart, and stitch pattern. Learn new approaches and hone your skills by experimenting with stitches on a small swatch. Many of my friends start projects, put them down, and never finish them because they become too frustrated. Don't worry about mistakes; you can easily correct them, and they become part of the learning curve, another step on your road to success as a knitter.

With proper preparation, you will be ready to knit any of these Twinkle patterns!

When you complete a project, and the design comes to life, you'll be showered with compliments and inspired to knit up something else.

KNITTING IN THE ROUND

We love going in circles! Knitting with short circular needles is modern and convenient. Circular needles fit into any hip handbag and travel everywhere. Since you don't need to join seams, you can knit all the way through without stopping.

Circular needles, available in many lengths, should be short enough to hold all your stitches without stretching them. I often use two circular needles to work on small necklines when the shortest circular needle is still too long. To accomplish this, divide the stitches evenly between two circular needles and knit with one circular needle at a time.

Although most patterns you'll find elsewhere are written for straight single-pointed needles, you can easily adjust the pattern for circular knitting. Here's some Twinkle Tips for adapting a flat pattern to a circular knit design:

- The right side is always facing you.
- When working on multiple stitch patterns, take out the stitches that are outside the repeat.
- Reverse wrong-side rows by reading the chart from right to left and making opposite stitches (for example, knit purl stitches and purl knit stitches).

CHILL WITH A CHUNKY

Often, I design sweaters just because I fall in love with a particular yarn. It could be anything about the yarn—texture, color, or even the challenge of not knowing how to design with it. When I first learned to knit, I enjoyed working with chunky yarn because it knits up fast. Now, I have grown to appreciate its many facets and capabilities.

Yarns have personality. The bulkier and softer the yarn, the more difficult it is to achieve consistency in gauge. Its inconsistencies add an artistic element to the design. Bulky yarn inherently appears stiffer. Through knitting, I work the flaws of chunky yarn to their advantage. For quirky, tiny sweaters, I like to exaggerate the bulk and pile it up, making cables, bobbles, or anything three-dimensional. Conversely, with lacy, open-weave patterns, I love creating intricate sheer effects that are perfect for lingerie or deconstructed looks.

Be adventurous with chunkies! Remake a pattern you like in rainbow stripes instead of solids. Revitalize an old design by using a heavier yarn and a larger needle. You will discover the joy of creating something unexpected from the familiar.

GO FOR IT WITH GAUGE

Gauge determines your design's measurements. Before knitting a sweater, make a swatch to ensure that you can achieve the correct gauge. If most of the garment is to be made in a pattern stitch, make a swatch in that pattern stitch.

For chunkies, the stitch gauge is fewer than three stitches to an inch (2.5cm), so exact gauge is crucial. For accuracy, I suggest making a larger swatch and measuring from the middle. Make it match: If your gauge does not match the example precisely, use a larger or smaller needle until it's right.

Some knitters notice that when knitting in the round, their tension is tighter. You might find that your gauge is different from the swatch knit flat on straight needles. Work on a gauge swatch in the round to know for sure.

KNITTING TECHNIQUES

Stockinette Stitch

Knit right-side rows;
purl wrong-side rows.

Stockinette Stitch in the Round

Knit all rounds.

Reverse Stockinette Stitch

Purl right-side rows;
knit wrong-side rows.

Reverse Stockinette Stitch in the Round

Purl all rounds.

Garter Stitch

Knit all rows.

Garter Stitch in the Round

RND 1: Knit.
RND 2: Purl.

Seed Stitch

ROW/RND 1: ★K1, p1; repeat from ★.
ROW/RND 2: Purl the knit stitches and knit the purl stitches.
Repeat Row/Rnd 2 for pattern.

K1, p1 rib

ROW/RND 1: ★K1, p1; repeat from ★.
ROW/RND 2: Knit the knit stitches and purl the purl stitches.
Repeat Row/Rnd 2 for pattern.

K2, p2 Rib

ROW/RND 1: ★K2, p2; repeat from ★.
ROW/RND 2: Knit the knit stitches and purl the purl stitches.
Repeat Row/Rnd 2 for pattern.

Attaching Fringe

Holding two or more strands together, fold strands in half. Insert crochet hook from back to front of garment edge and pull doubled strands through. Draw yarn ends through loop and pull tight (see illus. 1).

1

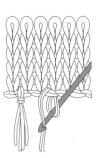

Increases and Decreases

Most increases and decreases should be fully fashioned. In other words, whenever possible they should be made one stitch away from the edge of the fabric, or from the stitch markers, according to the pattern.

Joining Stitches

- On circular needles (illus. 1).
- On double-pointed needles (illus. 2).
- Make sure stitches are not twisted when you're joining.

1

2

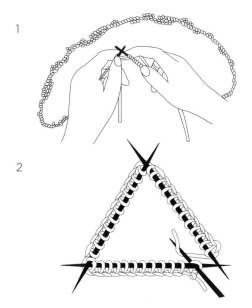

Making Buttonholes

- When you make a buttonhole with chunky yarn, binding off one stitch may be sufficient.
- For lighter-weight yarn, bind off more stitches, based on the button size (illus. 1).
- On next row, use the e-loop method to cast on the same number of stitches that were bound off on the previous row (illus. 2).

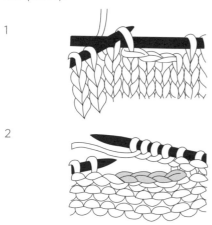

Markers

- Using markers is extremely important when you're knitting in the round (illus. 1 and 2).
- Used on the sides, center, front, and back, markers enable you to keep track of the beginning and the end.

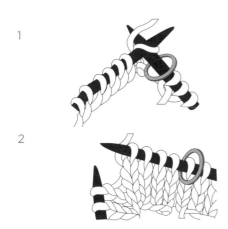

Picking Up Stitches

- On vertical edges, pick up one stitch in between each row (illus. 1 and 2).
- On horizontal edges, pick up one stitch in between each stitch (illus. 3 and 4).
- On slanted edges, pick up using the vertical or horizontal techniques described above (illus. 5)

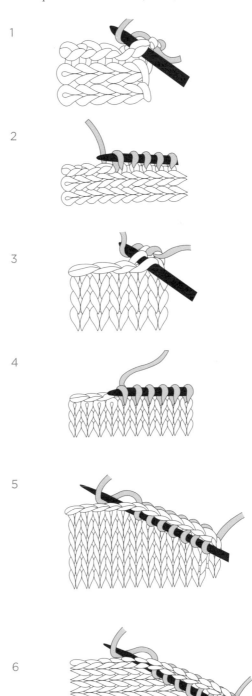

Seaming/Sewing

To seam finished pieces in stockinette stitch or reverse stockinette stitch together, select from the techniques outlined below.

- To get started (illus. 1), insert needle from the back (WS) to the front (RS) in the corner stitches of each piece you want to sew together. Pull tightly to close the gap.
- For vertical seams on stockinette stitch (illus. 2), use mattress stitch: Insert needle under the horizontal bar created by the edge stitch and the stitch next to it. Pull the yarn through and insert the needle into the corresponding bar on the opposite piece. Continue to work back and forth.
- For vertical seams on reverse stockinette stitch (illus. 3), insert needle into the loop created by the edge stitch. Pull the yarn through and insert the needle into the bottom loop of the corresponding stitch on the opposite piece. Continue to work back and forth.
- For horizontal seams in stockinette stitch (illus. 4), insert needle under a stitch inside the bound-off edge of one side. Pull yarn through and insert the needle under the corresponding stitch on the opposite side.
- For vertical-to-horizontal seams (illus. 5), insert needle under a stitch inside the bound-off edge of the horizontal piece. Pull through and insert needle under the horizontal bar between the first and second stitch of the vertical piece.

Short Rows

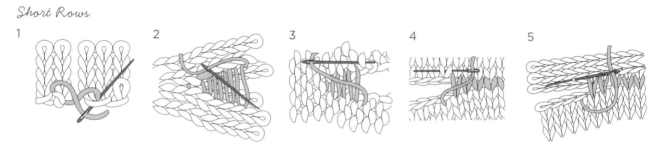

Short rows are made by working part of the way across a row, then turning and working back. However, in order to avoid a hole, you must "wrap" each stitch at the turning point. To wrap a stitch when the last stitch worked is a knit stitch: Knit to the turning point, slip next stitch onto right-hand needle purlwise (illus.1), bring yarn between needles (illus.2), slip stitch onto left-hand needle (illus.3), turn. Work in a similar manner when on the purl side (illus.4-5).

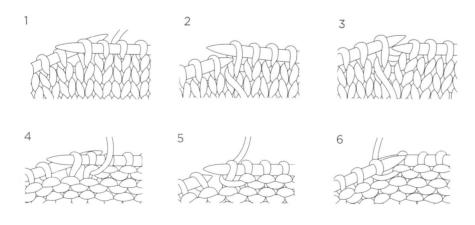

Three-Needle Bind-Off

Hold pieces to be joined with wrong sides together, needles parallel to each other and pointing to the right.

1. Insert right-hand needle into the first stitch on the front needle and into the first stitch on the back needle, and knit these two stitches together. One stitch is now on the right-hand needle.
2. Knit together the next pair of stitches in the same way.
3. Slip the first stitch on the right needle over the second stitch to bind it off.
4. Repeat the last two steps until one stitch remains on needle. Fasten off.

Using Stitch Holders

Try using waste yarn as a holder to keep from squeezing many stitches onto a small stitch holder.

Standard Yarn Weight System

YARN WEIGHT SYMBOL AND CATEGORY NAMES	2 FINE	6 SUPER BULKY
TYPES OF YARN IN CATEGORY	SPORT, BABY	BULKY, ROVING
KNIT GAUGE RANGE* IN STOCKINETTE STITCH TO 4 INCHES (10 CM)	23–26 sts	6–11 sts
RECOMMENDED NEEDLE IN METRIC SIZE RANGE	3.25–3.75 mm	8 mm and larger
RECOMMENDED NEEDLE IN U.S. SIZE RANGE	3 to 5	11 and larger

Twinkle Knit Bit

Twinkle knit garments adapt to a variety of outfits, but sometimes you want to see the colors you're trying to coordinate side-by-side. A wallet holding samples of yarns used in knitting projects is a great resource when shopping for clothes or yarn. A plastic checkbook cover that has a leaf for slipping between the check-and-carbon pair and the remaining stack of checks is ideal. Use a hole punch to perforate, with regularly spaced holes, the open edge of the leaf. Then, fold each yarn sample in half and poke the loop through the hole, pulling the loose ends through the loop as if to attach fringe. If you don't have extra yarn used for a garment, trim a woven-in end or tail from a seam on the knit itself. There's usually room left in the wallet for fabric swatches, yarn bands, business cards, or size charts as well. When you breeze into a resort boutique or LYS (local yarn shop), pull out your wallet and compare with confidence.

abbreviations

Ch   chain

C4L   (cable 4 left) slip next 2 stitches to a cable needle and hold in front of work, k2, k2 from the cable needle

K   knit

K1f&b   knit into the front and back of next stitch

K2tog   knit 2 together

MB   (make bobble) [k1, p1, k1] into next stitch, turn; p3, turn; k3tog

M1-L   make 1 increase, left-leaning—on the knit side: insert tip of left needle from front to back into the strand running between the two needles, lift this strand onto left needle, insert right needle into back of loop and knit.

M1-R   make 1 increase, right-leaning—on the knit side: insert tip of left needle from back to front into the strand running between the two needles; lift this strand onto left needle, insert right needle into front of loop and knit.

M1-p   make 1 increase purlwise—insert tip of left hand needle from back to front into the strand running between the two needles, lift this strand onto left hand needle, insert right hand needle purlwise into the front of the strand and purl it.

P   purl

P2tog   (purl 2 together) creates a right-leaning decrease on the purl side of the fabric

Rnd   round

RS   right side

Sm   slip marker

Ssk   (slip, slip, knit) slip next 2 stitches one at a time knitwise, insert the left-hand needle into both stitches as if to knit, knit those two stitches together—creates a right-leaning decrease

Sssk   (slip, slip, slip, knit) slip next 3 stitches one at a time knitwise, insert the left-hand needle into both stitches as if to knit, knit those three stitches together—creates a right-leaning decrease

Ssp   (slip, slip, purl) slip next 2 stitches one at a time knitwise to the right-hand needle, pass them back together to the left-hand needle, purl those two stitches together through back loop

Sssp   (slip, slip, slip, purl) slip next 2 stitches one at a time knitwise to the right-hand needle, pass them back together to the left-hand needle, purl those three stitches together through back loop

Tbl   through back loop

S2kp2   slip next 2 stitches together knitwise, knit next stitch, pass 2 slipped stitches over—creates a centered double decrease.

WS   wrong side

yo   (yarn over) bring the yarn over the needle.

yarn resources

Please visit the Twinkle Living website (www.twinkleliving.com) or the Twinkle by Wenlan website (www.twinklebywenlan.com) for stores near you that carry Twinkle yarns.

YARN SUBSTITUTION

Along with the sweaters in this book, I've designed the yarns they're worked in. Soft Chunky, Kids Mohair, and Cruise were created to deliver the look and feel I wanted in my designs. For the best results—the perfect shape, the perfect drape, the perfect fit, and the right amount of give—I suggest you use the specific yarns called for in the patterns.

However, if you want to substitute a different yarn for the Twinkle variety, be sure the fiber content, gauge, and overall yarn characteristics are the same. Here are suggestions for yarns that have a gauge and fiber content similar to the ones used. Please keep in mind that I have not tested these yarns myself, and they may create a sweater different in look and feel from the one pictured.

 *For Soft Chunky, try—*
Magnum from Cascade
Bulky Lopi from JCA
Baby from Tahki Stacy Charles
When substituting for Kids Mohair and Cruise, you may need to experiment
with the number of strands needed to meet the gauge.

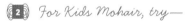 *For Kids Mohair, try—*
Lace Mohair from Karabella
Baby Kid Extra from Filatura di Crosa, distributed by Tahki Stacy Charles

 *For Cruise, try—*
Cotton Bamboo from Classic Elite Yarn
Cotton Fine from Brown Sheep Company
Breeze from Crystal Palace

acknowledgments

This book was made possible by the contributions of many talented and dedicated people. My sincerest thanks go out to those whose combined efforts resulted in beautiful book.

Rosy Ngo and Erin Slonaker, along with everyone else at my publisher, Potter Craft, deserve my profound gratitude for their support, trust, and patience throughout the process of making *Twinkle's Town & Country Knits*.

A heartfelt thank you goes to Caroline Greeven of the Agency Group for her constant encouragement and attention to this book.

To Edie Eckman, I owe a debt of thanks for her vast knitting expertise and skillful attention to my patterns. Charlotte Quiggle earned my appreciation with her keen sensitivity to design, details, and schedules. Thank you for a job well done.

The steadfast team that accompanied me on the memorable photo shoot for this book merits perhaps my heartiest thanks. Without the talents of each member of the team, *Twinkle's Town & Country Knits* would not contain the beautiful photographs and words that it does. Michael Crouser deserves my gratitude for his keen eye and tireless determination to create the perfect image; Sharon Anderson, for her artful, prescient vision that inspired me in this and in all artistic pursuits; John Haffner Layden for his bookmaking wisdom and temperate, get-the-job-done disposition; Sara Gelman and David Cruz for their artistry in creating, in makeup and hair, the fresh, charming look of the Twinkle models; Martina Correa, Ciara Nugent, and Hanne Gaby Odiele for their sunny smiles, elegant poses, and unwavering patience; and, finally, Leon Singleton and Soobin Sunwoo, for the enthusiasm and dedication they brought to each aspect of their work. I'd like to recognize Suzanne Quinn of Glow Communications and Jessica Longshore of NARS for their longstanding assistance. Roger and Mauricio Padilha of MAO also deserve thanks for rising to the occasion once more. The advice of experienced knitters Tiffany Chang, Anne Barker, Kathi Ferrara, Monique Nijhout, Kellie Overbey, Kate Sonnick, Vittoria Curl, Ivete Tecedor, Yolanda Finley, Jeanne Vagnetti, Nicole Hindes, Seimi Huang, Joanyuan Lee, Yu Yun Lee, Nadira Adams, Lori Rozmus, Jennifer Litwin, and Tracy McManus improved this book, and for that they are owed my thanks.

I am blessed with an incredible staff. The talented efforts of Katherine Lum, Yuki Sekiya, Karina Peng, Huang Ruixiang, Lily Tran, and Leon Yuan nurtured this project, so I'd like to acknowledge them here. Warm thanks go out to my capable interns Crystal Wei and Annie Kao for expertly handling many tasks in support of this book. Thanks to Kenneth Kao for his professional advice.

By opening the doors of their stunning home to us, Richard Chang and Tina Lee lent beautiful backdrops to some of the photographs in this book. I thank them for their kind support and generosity. The management staffs of the Sands Point Reserve, the Port Washington Yacht Club, the Belmont Lake State Park, the Baxter Estates Pond, the Baltimore Design Group of Sands Point, and the Babylon Riding Center also get my heartfelt appreciation for accommodating our photo shoots and for providing such fitting environments for this collection of twinkle designs.

index

Page numbers in *italics* indicate photographs.